Mometrix

TEST PREPARATION

OSAT®

I0878867

Journalism (137) Secrets Study Guide

OSAT, CEOE, Oklahoma Subject Area Tests, and Certification Examinations for Oklahoma Educators are trademarks of the Office of Educational Quality and Accountability and Pearson Education, Inc. or its affiliate(s). This product was developed by Mometrix Test Preparation. It was not developed in connection with Pearson Education, Inc., nor was it reviewed, approved or endorsed by these agencies.

DEAR FUTURE EXAM SUCCESS STORY

First of all, **THANK YOU** for purchasing Mometrix study materials!

Second, congratulations! You are one of the few determined test-takers who are committed to doing whatever it takes to excel on your exam. **You have come to the right place.** We developed these study materials with one goal in mind: to deliver you the information you need in a format that's concise and easy to use.

In addition to optimizing your guide for the content of the test, we've outlined our recommended steps for breaking down the preparation process into small, attainable goals so you can make sure you stay on track.

We've also analyzed the entire test-taking process, identifying the most common pitfalls and showing how you can overcome them and be ready for any curveball the test throws you.

Standardized testing is one of the biggest obstacles on your road to success, which only increases the importance of doing well in the high-pressure, high-stakes environment of test day. Your results on this test could have a significant impact on your future, and this guide provides the information and practical advice to help you achieve your full potential on test day.

Your success is our success

We would love to hear from you! If you would like to share the story of your exam success or if you have any questions or comments in regard to our products, please contact us at **800-673-8175** or **support@mometrix.com**.

Thanks again for your business and we wish you continued success!

Sincerely,
The Mometrix Test Preparation Team

Need more help? Check out our flashcards at:
http://MometrixFlashcards.com/CEOE

Copyright © 2026 by Mometrix Media LLC. All rights reserved.
Written and edited by the Mometrix Exam Secrets Test Prep Team
Printed in the United States of America

TABLE OF CONTENTS

Introduction

Thank you for purchasing this resource! You have made the choice to prepare yourself for a test that could have a huge impact on your future, and this guide is designed to help you be fully ready for test day. Obviously, it's important to have a solid understanding of the test material, but you also need to be prepared for the unique environment and stressors of the test, so that you can perform to the best of your abilities.

For this purpose, the first section that appears in this guide is the **Secret Keys**. We've devoted countless hours to meticulously researching what works and what doesn't, and we've boiled down our findings to the five most impactful steps you can take to improve your performance on the test. We start at the beginning with study planning and move through the preparation process, all the way to the testing strategies that will help you get the most out of what you know when you're finally sitting in front of the test.

We recommend that you start preparing for your test as far in advance as possible. However, if you've bought this guide as a last-minute study resource and only have a few days before your test, we recommend that you skip over the first two Secret Keys since they address a long-term study plan.

If you struggle with **test anxiety**, we strongly encourage you to check out our recommendations for how you can overcome it. Test anxiety is a formidable foe, but it can be beaten, and we want to make sure you have the tools you need to defeat it.

Copyright © Mometrix Media. You have been licensed one copy of this document for personal use only. Any other reproduction or redistribution is strictly prohibited. All rights reserved.
This content is provided for test preparation purposes only and does not imply an endorsement by Mometrix of any particular political, scientific, or religious point of view.

Secret Key #1 – Plan Big, Study Small

There's a lot riding on your performance. If you want to ace this test, you're going to need to keep your skills sharp and the material fresh in your mind. You need a plan that lets you review everything you need to know while still fitting in your schedule. We'll break this strategy down into three categories.

Information Organization

Start with the information you already have: the official test outline. From this, you can make a complete list of all the concepts you need to cover before the test. Organize these concepts into groups that can be studied together, and create a list of any related vocabulary you need to learn so you can brush up on any difficult terms. You'll want to keep this vocabulary list handy once you actually start studying since you may need to add to it along the way.

Time Management

Once you have your set of study concepts, decide how to spread them out over the time you have left before the test. Break your study plan into small, clear goals so you have a manageable task for each day and know exactly what you're doing. Then just focus on one small step at a time. When you manage your time this way, you don't need to spend hours at a time studying. Studying a small block of content for a short period each day helps you retain information better and avoid stressing over how much you have left to do. You can relax knowing that you have a plan to cover everything in time. In order for this strategy to be effective though, you have to start studying early and stick to your schedule. Avoid the exhaustion and futility that comes from last-minute cramming!

Study Environment

The environment you study in has a big impact on your learning. Studying in a coffee shop, while probably more enjoyable, is not likely to be as fruitful as studying in a quiet room. It's important to keep distractions to a minimum. You're only planning to study for a short block of time, so make the most of it. Don't pause to check your phone or get up to find a snack. It's also important to **avoid multitasking**. Research has consistently shown that multitasking will make your studying dramatically less effective. Your study area should also be comfortable and well-lit so you don't have the distraction of straining your eyes or sitting on an uncomfortable chair.

The time of day you study is also important. You want to be rested and alert. Don't wait until just before bedtime. Study when you'll be most likely to comprehend and remember. Even better, if you know what time of day your test will be, set that time aside for study. That way your brain will be used to working on that subject at that specific time and you'll have a better chance of recalling information.

Finally, it can be helpful to team up with others who are studying for the same test. Your actual studying should be done in as isolated an environment as possible, but the work of organizing the information and setting up the study plan can be divided up. In between study sessions, you can discuss with your teammates the concepts that you're all studying and quiz each other on the details. Just be sure that your teammates are as serious about the test as you are. If you find that your study time is being replaced with social time, you might need to find a new team.

Copyright © Mometrix Media. You have been licensed one copy of this document for personal use only. Any other reproduction or redistribution is strictly prohibited. All rights reserved.
This content is provided for test preparation purposes only and does not imply an endorsement by Mometrix of any particular political, scientific, or religious point of view.

Secret Key #2 – Make Your Studying Count

You're devoting a lot of time and effort to preparing for this test, so you want to be absolutely certain it will pay off. This means doing more than just reading the content and hoping you can remember it on test day. It's important to make every minute of study count. There are two main areas you can focus on to make your studying count.

Retention

It doesn't matter how much time you study if you can't remember the material. You need to make sure you are retaining the concepts. To check your retention of the information you're learning, try recalling it at later times with minimal prompting. Try carrying around flashcards and glance at one or two from time to time or ask a friend who's also studying for the test to quiz you.

To enhance your retention, look for ways to put the information into practice so that you can apply it rather than simply recalling it. If you're using the information in practical ways, it will be much easier to remember. Similarly, it helps to solidify a concept in your mind if you're not only reading it to yourself but also explaining it to someone else. Ask a friend to let you teach them about a concept you're a little shaky on (or speak aloud to an imaginary audience if necessary). As you try to summarize, define, give examples, and answer your friend's questions, you'll understand the concepts better and they will stay with you longer. Finally, step back for a big picture view and ask yourself how each piece of information fits with the whole subject. When you link the different concepts together and see them working together as a whole, it's easier to remember the individual components.

Finally, practice showing your work on any multi-step problems, even if you're just studying. Writing out each step you take to solve a problem will help solidify the process in your mind, and you'll be more likely to remember it during the test.

Modality

Modality simply refers to the means or method by which you study. Choosing a study modality that fits your own individual learning style is crucial. No two people learn best in exactly the same way, so it's important to know your strengths and use them to your advantage.

For example, if you learn best by visualization, focus on visualizing a concept in your mind and draw an image or a diagram. Try color-coding your notes, illustrating them, or creating symbols that will trigger your mind to recall a learned concept. If you learn best by hearing or discussing information, find a study partner who learns the same way or read aloud to yourself. Think about how to put the information in your own words. Imagine that you are giving a lecture on the topic and record yourself so you can listen to it later.

For any learning style, flashcards can be helpful. Organize the information so you can take advantage of spare moments to review. Underline key words or phrases. Use different colors for different categories. Mnemonic devices (such as creating a short list in which every item starts with the same letter) can also help with retention. Find what works best for you and use it to store the information in your mind most effectively and easily.

Copyright © Mometrix Media. You have been licensed one copy of this document for personal use only. Any other reproduction or redistribution is strictly prohibited. All rights reserved.
This content is provided for test preparation purposes only and does not imply an endorsement by Mometrix of any particular political, scientific, or religious point of view.

Secret Key #3 – Practice the Right Way

Your success on test day depends not only on how many hours you put into preparing, but also on whether you prepared the right way. It's good to check along the way to see if your studying is paying off. One of the most effective ways to do this is by taking practice tests to evaluate your progress. Practice tests are useful because they show exactly where you need to improve. Every time you take a practice test, pay special attention to these three groups of questions:

- The questions you got wrong
- The questions you had to guess on, even if you guessed right
- The questions you found difficult or slow to work through

This will show you exactly what your weak areas are, and where you need to devote more study time. Ask yourself why each of these questions gave you trouble. Was it because you didn't understand the material? Was it because you didn't remember the vocabulary? Do you need more repetitions on this type of question to build speed and confidence? Dig into those questions and figure out how you can strengthen your weak areas as you go back to review the material.

Additionally, many practice tests have a section explaining the answer choices. It can be tempting to read the explanation and think that you now have a good understanding of the concept. However, an explanation likely only covers part of the question's broader context. Even if the explanation makes perfect sense, **go back and investigate** every concept related to the question until you're positive you have a thorough understanding.

As you go along, keep in mind that the practice test is just that: practice. Memorizing these questions and answers will not be very helpful on the actual test because it is unlikely to have any of the same exact questions. If you only know the right answers to the sample questions, you won't be prepared for the real thing. **Study the concepts** until you understand them fully, and then you'll be able to answer any question that shows up on the test.

It's important to wait on the practice tests until you're ready. If you take a test on your first day of study, you may be overwhelmed by the amount of material covered and how much you need to learn. Work up to it gradually.

On test day, you'll need to be prepared for answering questions, managing your time, and using the test-taking strategies you've learned. It's a lot to balance, like a mental marathon that will have a big impact on your future. Like training for a marathon, you'll need to start slowly and work your way up. When test day arrives, you'll be ready.

Start with the strategies you've read in the first two Secret Keys—plan your course and study in the way that works best for you. If you have time, consider using multiple study resources to get different approaches to the same concepts. It can be helpful to see difficult concepts from more than one angle. Then find a good source for practice tests. Many times, the test website will suggest potential study resources or provide sample tests.

Copyright © Mometrix Media. You have been licensed one copy of this document for personal use only. Any other reproduction or redistribution is strictly prohibited. All rights reserved.
This content is provided for test preparation purposes only and does not imply an endorsement by Mometrix of any particular political, scientific, or religious point of view.

Practice Test Strategy

If you're able to find at least three practice tests, we recommend this strategy:

Untimed and Open-Book Practice

Take the first test with no time constraints and with your notes and study guide handy. Take your time and focus on applying the strategies you've learned.

Timed and Open-Book Practice

Take the second practice test open-book as well, but set a timer and practice pacing yourself to finish in time.

Timed and Closed-Book Practice

Take any other practice tests as if it were test day. Set a timer and put away your study materials. Sit at a table or desk in a quiet room, imagine yourself at the testing center, and answer questions as quickly and accurately as possible.

Keep repeating timed and closed-book tests on a regular basis until you run out of practice tests or it's time for the actual test. Your mind will be ready for the schedule and stress of test day, and you'll be able to focus on recalling the material you've learned.

Copyright © Mometrix Media. You have been licensed one copy of this document for personal use only. Any other reproduction or redistribution is strictly prohibited. All rights reserved.
This content is provided for test preparation purposes only and does not imply an endorsement by Mometrix of any particular political, scientific, or religious point of view.

Secret Key #4 – Pace Yourself

Once you're fully prepared for the material on the test, your biggest challenge on test day will be managing your time. Just knowing that the clock is ticking can make you panic even if you have plenty of time left. Work on pacing yourself so you can build confidence against the time constraints of the exam. Pacing is a difficult skill to master, especially in a high-pressure environment, so **practice is vital**.

Set time expectations for your pace based on how much time is available. For example, if a section has 60 questions and the time limit is 30 minutes, you know you have to average 30 seconds or less per question in order to answer them all. Although 30 seconds is the hard limit, set 25 seconds per question as your goal, so you reserve extra time to spend on harder questions. When you budget extra time for the harder questions, you no longer have any reason to stress when those questions take longer to answer.

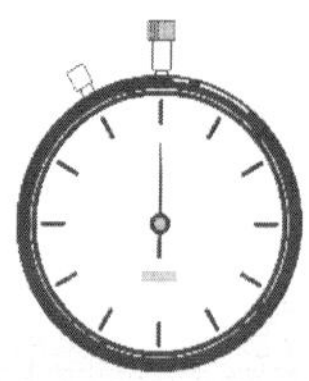

Don't let this time expectation distract you from working through the test at a calm, steady pace, but keep it in mind so you don't spend too much time on any one question. Recognize that taking extra time on one question you don't understand may keep you from answering two that you do understand later in the test. If your time limit for a question is up and you're still not sure of the answer, mark it and move on, and come back to it later if the time and the test format allow. If the testing format doesn't allow you to return to earlier questions, just make an educated guess; then put it out of your mind and move on.

On the easier questions, be careful not to rush. It may seem wise to hurry through them so you have more time for the challenging ones, but it's not worth missing one if you know the concept and just didn't take the time to read the question fully. Work efficiently but make sure you understand the question and have looked at all of the answer choices, since more than one may seem right at first.

Even if you're paying attention to the time, you may find yourself a little behind at some point. You should speed up to get back on track, but do so wisely. Don't panic; just take a few seconds less on each question until you're caught up. Don't guess without thinking, but do look through the answer choices and eliminate any you know are wrong. If you can get down to two choices, it is often worthwhile to guess from those. Once you've chosen an answer, move on and don't dwell on any that you skipped or had to hurry through. If a question was taking too long, chances are it was one of the harder ones, so you weren't as likely to get it right anyway.

On the other hand, if you find yourself getting ahead of schedule, it may be beneficial to slow down a little. The more quickly you work, the more likely you are to make a careless mistake that will affect your score. You've budgeted time for each question, so don't be afraid to spend that time. Practice an efficient but careful pace to get the most out of the time you have.

Copyright © Mometrix Media. You have been licensed one copy of this document for personal use only. Any other reproduction or redistribution is strictly prohibited. All rights reserved.
This content is provided for test preparation purposes only and does not imply an endorsement by Mometrix of any particular political, scientific, or religious point of view.

Secret Key #5 – Have a Plan for Guessing

When you're taking the test, you may find yourself stuck on a question. Some of the answer choices seem better than others, but you don't see the one answer choice that is obviously correct. What do you do?

The scenario described above is very common, yet most test takers have not effectively prepared for it. Developing and practicing a plan for guessing may be one of the single most effective uses of your time as you get ready for the exam.

In developing your plan for guessing, there are three questions to address:

- When should you start the guessing process?
- How should you narrow down the choices?
- Which answer should you choose?

When to Start the Guessing Process

Unless your plan for guessing is to select C every time (which, despite its merits, is not what we recommend), you need to leave yourself enough time to apply your answer elimination strategies. Since you have a limited amount of time for each question, that means that if you're going to give yourself the best shot at guessing correctly, you have to decide quickly whether or not you will guess.

Of course, the best-case scenario is that you don't have to guess at all, so first, see if you can answer the question based on your knowledge of the subject and basic reasoning skills. Focus on the key words in the question and try to jog your memory of related topics. Give yourself a chance to bring the knowledge to mind, but once you realize that you don't have (or you can't access) the knowledge you need to answer the question, it's time to start the guessing process.

It's almost always better to start the guessing process too early than too late. It only takes a few seconds to remember something and answer the question from knowledge. Carefully eliminating wrong answer choices takes longer. Plus, going through the process of eliminating answer choices can actually help jog your memory.

Summary: Start the guessing process as soon as you decide that you can't answer the question based on your knowledge.

Copyright © Mometrix Media. You have been licensed one copy of this document for personal use only. Any other reproduction or redistribution is strictly prohibited. All rights reserved.
This content is provided for test preparation purposes only and does not imply an endorsement by Mometrix of any particular political, scientific, or religious point of view.

How to Narrow Down the Choices

The next chapter in this book (**Test-Taking Strategies**) includes a wide range of strategies for how to approach questions and how to look for answer choices to eliminate. You will definitely want to read those carefully, practice them, and figure out which ones work best for you. Here though, we're going to address a mindset rather than a particular strategy.

Your odds of guessing an answer correctly depend on how many options you are choosing from.

Number of options left	5	4	3	2	1
Odds of guessing correctly	20%	25%	33%	50%	100%

You can see from this chart just how valuable it is to be able to eliminate incorrect answers and make an educated guess, but there are two things that many test takers do that cause them to miss out on the benefits of guessing:

- Accidentally eliminating the correct answer
- Selecting an answer based on an impression

We'll look at the first one here, and the second one in the next section.

To avoid accidentally eliminating the correct answer, we recommend a thought exercise called **the $5 challenge**. In this challenge, you only eliminate an answer choice from contention if you are willing to bet $5 on it being wrong. Why $5? Five dollars is a small but not insignificant amount of money. It's an amount you could afford to lose but wouldn't want to throw away. And while losing $5 once might not hurt too much, doing it twenty times will set you back $100. In the same way, each small decision you make—eliminating a choice here, guessing on a question there—won't by itself impact your score very much, but when you put them all together, they can make a big difference. By holding each answer choice elimination decision to a higher standard, you can reduce the risk of accidentally eliminating the correct answer.

The $5 challenge can also be applied in a positive sense: If you are willing to bet $5 that an answer choice *is* correct, go ahead and mark it as correct.

Summary: Only eliminate an answer choice if you are willing to bet $5 that it is wrong.

Copyright © Mometrix Media. You have been licensed one copy of this document for personal use only. Any other reproduction or redistribution is strictly prohibited. All rights reserved.
This content is provided for test preparation purposes only and does not imply an endorsement by Mometrix of any particular political, scientific, or religious point of view.

Which Answer to Choose

You're taking the test. You've run into a hard question and decided you'll have to guess. You've eliminated all the answer choices you're willing to bet $5 on. Now you have to pick an answer. Why do we even need to talk about this? Why can't you just pick whichever one you feel like when the time comes?

The answer to these questions is that if you don't come into the test with a plan, you'll rely on your impression to select an answer choice, and if you do that, you risk falling into a trap. The test writers know that everyone who takes their test will be guessing on some of the questions, so they intentionally write wrong answer choices to seem plausible. You still have to pick an answer though, and if the wrong answer choices are designed to look right, how can you ever be sure that you're not falling for their trap? The best solution we've found to this dilemma is to take the decision out of your hands entirely. Here is the process we recommend:

Once you've eliminated any choices that you are confident (willing to bet $5) are wrong, select the first remaining choice as your answer.

Whether you choose to select the first remaining choice, the second, or the last, the important thing is that you use some preselected standard. Using this approach guarantees that you will not be enticed into selecting an answer choice that looks right, because you are not basing your decision on how the answer choices look.

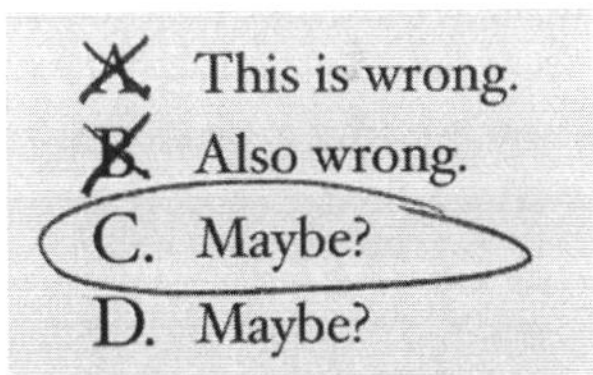

This is not meant to make you question your knowledge. Instead, it is to help you recognize the difference between your knowledge and your impressions. There's a huge difference between thinking an answer is right because of what you know, and thinking an answer is right because it looks or sounds like it should be right.

Summary: To ensure that your selection is appropriately random, make a predetermined selection from among all answer choices you have not eliminated.

Copyright © Mometrix Media. You have been licensed one copy of this document for personal use only. Any other reproduction or redistribution is strictly prohibited. All rights reserved.
This content is provided for test preparation purposes only and does not imply an endorsement by Mometrix of any particular political, scientific, or religious point of view.

Test-Taking Strategies

This section contains a list of test-taking strategies that you may find helpful as you work through the test. By taking what you know and applying logical thought, you can maximize your chances of answering any question correctly!

It is very important to realize that every question is different and every person is different: no single strategy will work on every question, and no single strategy will work for every person. That's why we've included all of them here, so you can try them out and determine which ones work best for different types of questions and which ones work best for you.

Question Strategies

✓ Read Carefully

Read the question and the answer choices carefully. Don't miss the question because you misread the terms. You have plenty of time to read each question thoroughly and make sure you understand what is being asked. Yet a happy medium must be attained, so don't waste too much time. You must read carefully and efficiently.

✓ Contextual Clues

Look for contextual clues. If the question includes a word you are not familiar with, look at the immediate context for some indication of what the word might mean. Contextual clues can often give you all the information you need to decipher the meaning of an unfamiliar word. Even if you can't determine the meaning, you may be able to narrow down the possibilities enough to make a solid guess at the answer to the question.

✓ Prefixes

If you're having trouble with a word in the question or answer choices, try dissecting it. Take advantage of every clue that the word might include. Prefixes can be a huge help. Usually, they allow you to determine a basic meaning. *Pre-* means before, *post-* means after, *pro-* is positive, *de-* is negative. From prefixes, you can get an idea of the general meaning of the word and try to put it into context.

✓ Hedge Words

Watch out for critical hedge words, such as *likely, may, can, often, almost, mostly, usually, generally, rarely,* and *sometimes.* Question writers insert these hedge phrases to cover every possibility. Often an answer choice will be wrong simply because it leaves no room for exception. Be on guard for answer choices that have definitive words such as *exactly* and *always.*

✓ Switchback Words

Stay alert for *switchbacks.* These are the words and phrases frequently used to alert you to shifts in thought. The most common switchback words are *but, although,* and *however.* Others include *nevertheless, on the other hand, even though, while, in spite of, despite,* and *regardless of.* Switchback words are important to catch because they can change the direction of the question or an answer choice.

Copyright © Mometrix Media. You have been licensed one copy of this document for personal use only. Any other reproduction or redistribution is strictly prohibited. All rights reserved.
This content is provided for test preparation purposes only and does not imply an endorsement by Mometrix of any particular political, scientific, or religious point of view.

⊘ Face Value

When in doubt, use common sense. Accept the situation in the problem at face value. Don't read too much into it. These problems will not require you to make wild assumptions. If you have to go beyond creativity and warp time or space in order to have an answer choice fit the question, then you should move on and consider the other answer choices. These are normal problems rooted in reality. The applicable relationship or explanation may not be readily apparent, but it is there for you to figure out. Use your common sense to interpret anything that isn't clear.

Answer Choice Strategies

⊘ Answer Selection

The most thorough way to pick an answer choice is to identify and eliminate wrong answers until only one is left, then confirm it is the correct answer. Sometimes an answer choice may immediately seem right, but be careful. The test writers will usually put more than one reasonable answer choice on each question, so take a second to read all of them and make sure that the other choices are not equally obvious. As long as you have time left, it is better to read every answer choice than to pick the first one that looks right without checking the others.

⊘ Answer Choice Families

An answer choice family consists of two (in rare cases, three) answer choices that are very similar in construction and cannot all be true at the same time. If you see two answer choices that are direct opposites or parallels, one of them is usually the correct answer. For instance, if one answer choice says that quantity *x* increases and another either says that quantity *x* decreases (opposite) or says that quantity *y* increases (parallel), then those answer choices would fall into the same family. An answer choice that doesn't match the construction of the answer choice family is more likely to be incorrect. Most questions will not have answer choice families, but when they do appear, you should be prepared to recognize them.

⊘ Eliminate Answers

Eliminate answer choices as soon as you realize they are wrong, but make sure you consider all possibilities. If you are eliminating answer choices and realize that the last one you are left with is also wrong, don't panic. Start over and consider each choice again. There may be something you missed the first time that you will realize on the second pass.

⊘ Avoid Fact Traps

Don't be distracted by an answer choice that is factually true but doesn't answer the question. You are looking for the choice that answers the question. Stay focused on what the question is asking for so you don't accidentally pick an answer that is true but incorrect. Always go back to the question and make sure the answer choice you've selected actually answers the question and is not merely a true statement.

⊘ Extreme Statements

In general, you should avoid answers that put forth extreme actions as standard practice or proclaim controversial ideas as established fact. An answer choice that states the "process should be used in certain situations, if…" is much more likely to be correct than one that states the "process should be discontinued completely." The first is a calm rational statement and doesn't even make a definitive, uncompromising stance, using a hedge word *if* to provide wiggle room, whereas the second choice is far more extreme.

Copyright © Mometrix Media. You have been licensed one copy of this document for personal use only. Any other reproduction or redistribution is strictly prohibited. All rights reserved.
This content is provided for test preparation purposes only and does not imply an endorsement by Mometrix of any particular political, scientific, or religious point of view.

✓ Benchmark

As you read through the answer choices and you come across one that seems to answer the question well, mentally select that answer choice. This is not your final answer, but it's the one that will help you evaluate the other answer choices. The one that you selected is your benchmark or standard for judging each of the other answer choices. Every other answer choice must be compared to your benchmark. That choice is correct until proven otherwise by another answer choice beating it. If you find a better answer, then that one becomes your new benchmark. Once you've decided that no other choice answers the question as well as your benchmark, you have your final answer.

✓ Predict the Answer

Before you even start looking at the answer choices, it is often best to try to predict the answer. When you come up with the answer on your own, it is easier to avoid distractions and traps because you will know exactly what to look for. The right answer choice is unlikely to be word-for-word what you came up with, but it should be a close match. Even if you are confident that you have the right answer, you should still take the time to read each option before moving on.

General Strategies

✓ Tough Questions

If you are stumped on a problem or it appears too hard or too difficult, don't waste time. Move on! Remember though, if you can quickly check for obviously incorrect answer choices, your chances of guessing correctly are greatly improved. Before you completely give up, at least try to knock out a couple of possible answers. Eliminate what you can and then guess at the remaining answer choices before moving on.

✓ Check Your Work

Since you will probably not know every term listed and the answer to every question, it is important that you get credit for the ones that you do know. Don't miss any questions through careless mistakes. If at all possible, try to take a second to look back over your answer selection and make sure you've selected the correct answer choice and haven't made a costly careless mistake (such as marking an answer choice that you didn't mean to mark). This quick double check should more than pay for itself in caught mistakes for the time it costs.

✓ Pace Yourself

It's easy to be overwhelmed when you're looking at a page full of questions; your mind is confused and full of random thoughts, and the clock is ticking down faster than you would like. Calm down and maintain the pace that you have set for yourself. Especially as you get down to the last few minutes of the test, don't let the small numbers on the clock make you panic. As long as you are on track by monitoring your pace, you are guaranteed to have time for each question.

✓ Don't Rush

It is very easy to make errors when you are in a hurry. Maintaining a fast pace in answering questions is pointless if it makes you miss questions that you would have gotten right otherwise. Test writers like to include distracting information and wrong answers that seem right. Taking a little extra time to avoid careless mistakes can make all the difference in your test score. Find a pace that allows you to be confident in the answers that you select.

Copyright © Mometrix Media. You have been licensed one copy of this document for personal use only. Any other reproduction or redistribution is strictly prohibited. All rights reserved.
This content is provided for test preparation purposes only and does not imply an endorsement by Mometrix of any particular political, scientific, or religious point of view.

⊘ Keep Moving

Panicking will not help you pass the test, so do your best to stay calm and keep moving. Taking deep breaths and going through the answer elimination steps you practiced can help to break through a stress barrier and keep your pace.

Final Notes

The combination of a solid foundation of content knowledge and the confidence that comes from practicing your plan for applying that knowledge is the key to maximizing your performance on test day. As your foundation of content knowledge is built up and strengthened, you'll find that the strategies included in this chapter become more and more effective in helping you quickly sift through the distractions and traps of the test to isolate the correct answer.

Now that you're preparing to move forward into the test content chapters of this book, be sure to keep your goal in mind. As you read, think about how you will be able to apply this information on the test. If you've already seen sample questions for the test and you have an idea of the question format and style, try to come up with questions of your own that you can answer based on what you're reading. This will give you valuable practice applying your knowledge in the same ways you can expect to on test day.

Good luck and good studying!

Copyright © Mometrix Media. You have been licensed one copy of this document for personal use only. Any other reproduction or redistribution is strictly prohibited. All rights reserved.
This content is provided for test preparation purposes only and does not imply an endorsement by Mometrix of any particular political, scientific, or religious point of view.

Copyright © Mometrix Media. You have been licensed one copy of this document for personal use only. Any other reproduction or redistribution is strictly prohibited. All rights reserved.
This content is provided for test preparation purposes only and does not imply an endorsement by Mometrix of any particular political, scientific, or religious point of view.

Journalism Skills and Processes

Forms of Journalistic Writing

Good Journalistic Writing

Good journalistic writing features short sentences and paragraphs, the use of active verbs, and the avoidance of jargon and vague words. Writers should keep their own opinions out of the story, and the instructor should promote the use of correct grammar and journalism style (e.g., Associated Press style). Other important skills include the ability to revise and edit copy with appropriate proofreading and copyediting symbols.

Inverted Pyramid

The inverted pyramid is a concise style of news writing characterized by presenting information in order from the most important facts to the least important. This style is also known as the "Five W's" because the opening paragraph includes the "who, what, when, where, and why" of the story.

This writing style is convenient for time-pressed readers; as such, even if the consumer does not read the article to its conclusion, the article includes sufficient detail for the reader to comprehend the information. Placing less-important facts at the end of the story also allows for quick editing without losing the main points of the story.

The inverted pyramid is a standard journalism format because it does two things very well: it quickly tells the reader what has happened, and it helps the reporter focus on key facts and identify them within the first few paragraphs.

On the other hand, the inverted pyramid does not lend itself to distinctive writing. This characteristic represents one of the drawbacks of this format for journalistic writing. The reporter may not have time to explain and support the opening paragraphs. In addition, space reasons are more likely to dictate deletion of information at the end of a story. Without the motivation to craft the article completely, reporters can fail to sustain their original momentum in many inverted-pyramid stories.

Narrative Approach

A narrative, also described as storytelling, features a story with a definite beginning, middle, and end; the reporter includes anecdotes and dialogue that build the story to a satisfying conclusion. Quotes within the story sound realistic, without the canned recitation of a press release.

Narration focuses on the people in the story, and their words and actions reveal their motives. This writing style works better with a feature story than with breaking news because of the time required to develop the narrative structure.

Hourglass Approach

The hourglass approach to writing a news story presents a hybrid of the narrative and the inverted-pyramid formats. The first part of the story employs the inverted pyramid format to communicate the basic facts. Next comes the "turn," a transitional device that introduces the narrative and gives the article a structured beginning, middle, and end.

Copyright © Mometrix Media. You have been licensed one copy of this document for personal use only. Any other reproduction or redistribution is strictly prohibited. All rights reserved.
This content is provided for test preparation purposes only and does not imply an endorsement by Mometrix of any particular political, scientific, or religious point of view.

As is the case with a narrative, the hourglass works best when reporters have time to develop a story beyond the basics. This approach is particularly effective with subjects that lend themselves to chronological telling (e.g., criminal trials, police stories, etc.).

The advantages of the hourglass format are that readers can ascertain the facts quickly, and journalists can tell a story creatively rather than merely reciting facts.

Persuasive Writing

Persuasive writing takes a position for or against an issue. As such, it attempts to convince a reader to take action.

This style is not a relevant choice for writing a straight news story, since the objective of straight news is to present both sides of an issue or an event without including a reporter's personal opinion. However, persuasive writing is useful when writing an editorial. In this context, reporters can make an effective case for their point of view by presenting facts to back up their opinions.

Hard News

Hard news articles are factual, time-sensitive accounts of recent events. These stories generally appear in the first few pages of the newspaper's national, local, and sports sections.

Feature News Article

Feature stories, also known as soft news, are longer-form articles and profiles about people, issues, and events. Analysis examines the reactions and impact of a hard-news story.

Editorials and Opinion Pieces

Editorials are a piece written as the official stance or opinion of a group or publisher regarding a particular issue or topic. An opinion piece is a piece written by an individual discussing their point of view on a particular issue or topic. These two can be easily confused because all editorials are opinion pieces, but not all opinion pieces are editorials.

Column

Straight news involves basic reporting; e.g., covering an issue and telling readers what happened. Columnists, by contrast, are essentially opinion writers. They tend to have a regular following of readers who feel they can gain knowledge and insight from the columnist's work.

Although often perceived as more interesting than writing straight news, writing a column also proves a more challenging style of writing. Writing a good column involves more than just expressing an opinion. It requires clear thinking and the ability to present the columnist's "case" to the readers. The columnist's opinions must be insightful, convincing, and entertaining.

Blogs

Blogs (short for "weblogs") are digital diaries that allow anyone with a computer and an online connection to comment on issues of the day. While many bloggers make no pretense of objectivity, their commentary supplements mainstream journalism often in an entertaining way. Bloggers also have served as the initial source for stories further developed by newspapers and the electronic media.

Copyright © Mometrix Media. You have been licensed one copy of this document for personal use only. Any other reproduction or redistribution is strictly prohibited. All rights reserved.
This content is provided for test preparation purposes only and does not imply an endorsement by Mometrix of any particular political, scientific, or religious point of view.

Examples of popular political blogs include The Huffington Post, the Daily Kos, and Breitbart.com.

Posting News Articles Online

A story posted on newspaper's website is likely to attract a wider audience. People who do not subscribe to the printed version of the paper can read the story online (usually at no cost).

Online journalism also adds a greater interactive element than is possible in print. Links to articles on related subjects often follow online stories, and readers can post and leave comments regarding the original article. Although further research and commentary is available after reading a printed story, the immediacy of online content makes such interaction much more convenient.

Review Video: Journals, Diaries, Letters, and Blogs
Visit mometrix.com/academy and enter code: 432845

Hard Sell Advertisement

Whether in print or electronic media, "hard sell" advertising takes a direct, aggressive sales approach. For example, a hard sell ad from a local car dealership might use time-sensitive wording and large, attention-grabbing headlines such as "Used Car Blowout, This Weekend Only!"

Soft Sell

Soft sell advertising has a subtle and casual message. While not as likely to produce the immediate reaction of a hard sell, soft-sell ads are less irritating and often can be more persuasive in the end.

A good example of soft-sell advertising is a recent campaign for John Hancock investments, in which the television commercial features images of text messages sent on smartphones and laptops in tandem with understated background noise and the sound of clicking keystrokes.

News Copy vs. Advertising Copy

News copy strives for balance, objectivity, and fairness. As such, a reporter never should include his or her opinion in the story.

On the other hand, advertising copy emphasizes a particular product or service. With its more positive and promotional tone, advertising copy seeks to increase sales for the product or service being promoted.

Citizen Journalism

Citizen journalism refers to the collection of news and information by individuals without formal journalism training.

Examples of citizen journalism include photos taken with a camera phone at a breaking-news scene, and blogs that cover local issues.

Photojournalism

Photojournalism

Like consumers of other products, the audience for journalism continues to grow more ethnically and racially diverse. Patronizing or offending these readers will drive them away from your publication.

Copyright © Mometrix Media. You have been licensed one copy of this document for personal use only. Any other reproduction or redistribution is strictly prohibited. All rights reserved.
This content is provided for test preparation purposes only and does not imply an endorsement by Mometrix of any particular political, scientific, or religious point of view.

Contrast

Refers to the degree of tones in an image. Since many student publications print in black-and-white, having the widest possible contrast range between "pure" black and "pure" white is important. Poorly printed photographs have too much of a grayish tone and give the page a muddy look, thereby making it less attractive to potential readers.

Technical Qualities

A published photograph must attract the reader's eye and visually draw him or her to that page. Good technical qualities include sufficient lighting as well as accurate reproduction of the negative during development.

An overexposed photograph will appear "washed out" in a publication because the image was exposed to too much light. The opposite is true for an underexposed photo—an image that lacks sufficient light will appear dark and muddy on the page. In both cases, these factors detract from the overall design of the publication.

Designing Photo Layouts

A good photo layout should complement the text of a story and include photos of various sizes. If photos extend across two pages of an issue, the images should be completely viewable, and not cut off by the space between the pages.

For photo layout planning and design, photographs often communicate some stories to readers better than words. The amount of advertising sold for a particular issue also can affect the number of photos that can be included.

Film Camera

- The **lens** draws light into the camera and focuses it on the film plane.
- The **shutter** opens and closes to control the length of time that light strikes the film. The most common types of shutter are the leaf shutter (located between or just behind the lens) and the focal plane shutter (located in front of the film plane).
- The **shutter** release is button that releases the shutter mechanism.
- The **film advance lever** moves the film from one frame to the next.
- The **aperture** expands or contracts to control the diameter of the opening through which light passes. Adjusting the f-stop ring on the lens determines the amount of light that comes through the aperture.
- The **viewfinder** is a small piece of glass through which the photographer looks to frame the photograph.

Digital Camera

While digital cameras share several components with standard film cameras (lenses, apertures, etc.), they also have many additional features.

These features include a liquid crystal display (LCD) that shows the photographer the result of the picture just taken. The LCD panel acts a miniature graphical-use interface. It allows the user to adjust all camera settings. It also can help preview and arrange photos through the storage of thumbnails of images taken with the camera.

A memory card slot accepts digital memory cards (these can include hundreds of images on one card). A USB port allows the camera to connect to a computer via a USB cable. When the camera is

Copyright © Mometrix Media. You have been licensed one copy of this document for personal use only. Any other reproduction or redistribution is strictly prohibited. All rights reserved.
This content is provided for test preparation purposes only and does not imply an endorsement by Mometrix of any particular political, scientific, or religious point of view.

connected to a computer, the user can view and edit images on the computer screen. A docking port can be used to transfer photos, recharge batteries, and make prints.

Matte and Glossy Paper Stock

Matte paper has a non-reflective, non-textured surface. Glossy paper is coated with a compound (usually kaolinite or calcium carbonate) that gives the paper a shiny finish.

Magazines and similar publications commonly use glossy paper; matte paper tends to be used to reproduce fine art. Photographs and graphics appear differently when reproduced on the two papers. For student publications, glossy paper is likely choice for a yearbook or literary magazine. Matte paper tends to give images an understated look; in comparison, glossy stock tends to make image "pop" off the page.

Electronic Technology

Digital photography offers a several ways to manipulate, reproduce, and transmit images. The editing process for digital photography represents one of the biggest differences between film and digital photography. Instead of waiting for film to be developed, photojournalists working in a digital format can see the results of their work immediately. Such immediacy reduces the time required to find the best images to accompany a story.

Technology also is extending deadlines. By combining digital cameras, mobile phones, and laptop computers, scanning and transmitting photographs from the field to the newsroom can occur in mere minutes.

Manipulating Light

The amount of light required for a photograph depends on the location and the time of day. Pictures taken indoors or at night often require flash photography. Outdoor sports photography utilizes a flash to freeze action.

At the same time, use of flash photography should be judicious. In fact, using either indirect flash or no flash at all often can compose a more dramatic photograph. A direct flash also generates harsh shadows, which can create an unflattering image when photographing people.

When possible, a photographer should consider the time of day, especially for outdoor photography. Shadows are more dramatic in the early morning and late afternoon; as a result, a photo taken at 12 noon will have "flatter" light and thereby suffer by comparison.

Manual Camera Controls

Technological advances such as electronic flash and autofocus have made commercial cameras almost foolproof. However, knowledge of manual controls can help a photojournalist create a dramatic image far more memorable than a mere snapshot.

A slower f-stop can create a blurring action (e.g., a person running across the image) within an otherwise sharp print. In addition, calculating the available light, slowing down the shutter speed, and carefully holding the camera steady can help a photographer avoid using the flash.

Darkroom Chemicals

Darkroom chemicals usually are packaged as either a powder or a liquid concentrate. Powders tend to be less expensive and bulky; however, they dissolve more slowly in water, and some of the powder can become airborne when mixed.

Copyright © Mometrix Media. You have been licensed one copy of this document for personal use only. Any other reproduction or redistribution is strictly prohibited. All rights reserved.
This content is provided for test preparation purposes only and does not imply an endorsement by Mometrix of any particular political, scientific, or religious point of view.

Chemicals should be mixed in a well-ventilated area and then stored carefully in clean bottles or jugs. Containers should be dark or opaque, since the chemicals are sensitive to light. Plastic bottles are preferable to glass, since a plastic bottle will not break if dropped. This is an important consideration, since these bottles will be handled (literally) in the dark.

Because darkroom chemicals leach oxygen, a large jug can go bad sitting on the shelf. To slow down the oxygenation process, chemicals should be stored in small, dark bottles (16 to 20 ounces is best). In addition, keep bottles tightly capped and as full as possible in order to prevent air from entering the bottle.

Cropping Prints

Cropping is useful when a portion of a photo negative needs to be enlarged, or when extraneous items within the negative detract from the overall image.

To crop a print in the darkroom, raise the head of the enlarger until only the portion of the negative you wish to print is visible. The enlarger will have to be re-focused and the exposure time and f-stop will change, because the enlarger lamp is further from the printing paper and the light striking the page is less intense.

Stop Bath and Fixer

The stop bath is the second step in the development process. It lowers the pH value of the developer on the film; once the value drops below a certain threshold, the developer stops working. The most common stop bath is acetic acid, sold in concentrate form. Fixer is the final step in the process; it gives the photo a finished appearance. A wetting agent also can be used to squeegee any remaining liquid and reduce the chance of having water spots on the print.

Photograph's Interest and Effectiveness

Factors such as the content, composition, and technical qualities of a photograph determine whether a student newspaper should publish the photo. A particularly strong photo can fill front-page space, or an image that complements a front-page story can be placed on the "jump page."

Film Selection

Even with advancements in color and digital photography, most student newspapers continue to print photographs in black-and-white due to cost considerations.

While no single film serves all purposes, two good black-and-white film speeds to consider are ASA 200 and ASA 400. ASA 400 captures most still and action shots while reproducing photographs with a finer grain. ASA 200, a slower film speed, is good for close-up photos.

Faster film speeds allow the photojournalist to shoot in lower light and at faster shutter speed. The tradeoff is that the photograph captured with a faster film speed has a more coarse grain than a slower film speed; subsequently, the faster film speed loses a certain amount of detail.

Fish-Eye Lens

A fish-eye lens is a wide-angle lens that uses a distorted perspective to produce an interesting photograph. In the 35mm format—the most common film format in photojournalism—a fish-eye lens is about 16mm in length.

A photograph taken with a fish-eye lens will appear curved at the edges. Such lenses allow photojournalists to get as close as possible to their subjects while still maintaining context in photograph composition. Fish-eye lenses capture dramatic action shots well. In baseball, for

Copyright © Mometrix Media. You have been licensed one copy of this document for personal use only. Any other reproduction or redistribution is strictly prohibited. All rights reserved.
This content is provided for test preparation purposes only and does not imply an endorsement by Mometrix of any particular political, scientific, or religious point of view.

example, a fish-eye lens can focus on the bat of a hitter standing in the batter's box and still pick up an image of the hitter.

TELEPHOTO LENS

A telephoto lens (also known as a "long lens") is literally longer than the standard lens used in the 35mm format. The telephoto length generally starts at 85mm, compared to the 50mm standard lens.

The telephoto lens magnifies distant objects, compresses the distance between the object and the camera, and narrows the overall field of vision.

Because of the narrow field of vision, a telephoto lens can blur the background and focus on the subject. Photographers commonly use telephoto lenses in sports photography in order to capture images in a specific area of the field or court. A close-up photo of a running back being tackled in a football game is best achieved with a telephoto lens.

WIDE-ANGLE LENS

In the 35mm format, a wide-angle lens has a shorter focal length (generally 24mm to 28mm) than the standard 50mm lens. This lens is arguably the most versatile lens in the photojournalist's bag; a photo taken with a wide-angle lens will appear more dramatic than one taken with a standard lens.

A wide-angle lens adds distance between the object and the camera and magnifies the depth of field. While the perspective distortion is less with a wide-angle lens than with a fish-eye lens, the larger angle of view will cause parallel lines to converge within the photo. One example of effective use of this technique occurs when photographing a high-rise building.

DODGING

Dodging is a technique that manipulates the exposure of certain areas within a photograph. The darkroom technician decreases the exposure of light to a certain area in order to lighten that specific area the effect is to lighten that specific area.

BURNING

When developing a photograph, burning is the opposite of dodging. Burning increases the exposure of light within a specific portion of the print in order to darken that area of the photograph. A photojournalist uses burning to add drama to elements within the overall image. In digital photography, the vignetting technique ("burning" the edges of a photograph) can be achieved by using special filters.

RULE OF THIRDS

The rule of thirds refers a visual concept that divides an image into nine parts by using two horizontal and two vertical lines. These lines cross the image one-third of the way up and down. The dominant subject in a photograph should appear at one of these intersecting lines (e.g., one-third to the left, right, up, or down from the center of the image). By placing the subject in this area, the photo creates a more interesting composition and attracts the viewer's eye.

Copyright © Mometrix Media. You have been licensed one copy of this document for personal use only. Any other reproduction or redistribution is strictly prohibited. All rights reserved.
This content is provided for test preparation purposes only and does not imply an endorsement by Mometrix of any particular political, scientific, or religious point of view.

Gathering Information

Sources

Stored sources are information found in written or electronic files. Reporters use stored sources in the early stages of developing a story; these kinds of sources are helpful especially when researching an investigative article.

Personal sources are people who provide journalists with information. These sources are important because timely information is essential for an effective news story.

Observational sources refer to information journalists witness in the course of their reporting. Sports stories frequently employ observational sourcing, in which a reporter will explain the ebb and flow of a basketball game, for example.

Primary Sources

For a deadline story, a primary source is a person who has direct knowledge of a situation or who actively participated in the event.

Primary sources provide essential information (the "who," "what," "when," "where," and "why") that will appear in a news story's opening paragraphs. Investigative journalists also use archives of public records as primary sources.

Secondary Sources

Secondary sources evaluate and interpret information obtained through a primary source. When a government document is issued (for example, the monthly US job report and unemployment rate), journalists often seek out economists and employment experts to explain the numbers and analyze what changes in those numbers mean.

Reporters must use care with secondary sources. Many sources interpret information through their own biases, which can distort the facts and undermine the objectivity that is a hallmark of good journalism.

Citing Sources

Reporters should identify specifically all sources within a news story, including name (and title, if applicable).

Furthermore, reporters should attribute quotes to the one who provided the quote. Such attribution should be clear. Reporters also should specify the manner in which they obtained information from the source (e.g., face-to-face interview, telephone conversation, e-mail reply).

Direct Quote

A direct quote is an exact, word-for-word report of what a person says. A direct quote always should be placed within quotation marks.

Quotes enliven a news story and make it more attractive to readers. However, they should be used only when they add color and humanity to the reporting. Devoting several paragraphs to a single quote can lessen the impact of a story and risks turning the news article into a transcript.

Copyright © Mometrix Media. You have been licensed one copy of this document for personal use only. Any other reproduction or redistribution is strictly prohibited. All rights reserved.
This content is provided for test preparation purposes only and does not imply an endorsement by Mometrix of any particular political, scientific, or religious point of view.

Indirect Quote

An indirect quote does not reproduce exactly a person's remarks, but it is faithful to the meaning of the remarks. Using indirect quotes in tandem with direct quotes can help maintain the flow and narrative of a news article.

Internet Material and Sources

Time constraints are unavoidable in the field of journalism. Reporters who access information online (e.g., text or a cartoon graphic) cannot use the material without proper credit. If time constraints prevent the reporter from the obtaining the necessary permission prior to deadline, the material cannot be used.

Listing a "pending" copyright notice with the online material can be interpreted as a violation of copyright law. Remember that the online source of the material may not be the actual copyright holder.

Using the Internet

Online research can serve as a good first step when researching a story. However, journalists should keep in mind that anyone with access to an Internet server could upload material to the Web.

As such, journalists should examine online information closely for accuracy. Articles from scholarly journals likely are reputable, since most journals require all articles to undergo peer review by experts in the field. Relying on blogs or personal websites can be risky, nonetheless; the quality and reliability of such sites can vary greatly.

Reliable Web Sites

In terms of the information presented, a reliable Web site is comprehensive and focused, and it presents a balanced viewpoint. The site should show evidence of recent updates and should feature ways to access content posted earlier (a search engine within the site is helpful).

In terms of its reliability, the site should be stable and should function well. It should work with a variety of Web browsers (e.g., Internet Explorer, Firefox, Safari), and all internal and external links should function properly. In addition, contact information (including names and addresses) for persons responsible for the site should be easy to access from the site.

Databases

Databases are organized collections of information often categorized according to content (e.g., bibliographic, statistical, document-text).

In order to find relevant information quickly, journalists should set clear definitions for their search subjects. A search can be expressed as a statement or a question. If more than one concept is included, use "or" to combine terms representing the same idea. Use "and" to combine different sets of terms representing that idea.

Evaluating information is an important step; even a library database such as Lexis-Nexus includes articles written with a certain amount of bias. The accuracy of research sources depends on the publisher of the material and whether an author's work is critiqued for accuracy.

Copyright © Mometrix Media. You have been licensed one copy of this document for personal use only. Any other reproduction or redistribution is strictly prohibited. All rights reserved.
This content is provided for test preparation purposes only and does not imply an endorsement by Mometrix of any particular political, scientific, or religious point of view.

Evaluating News Sources

Sources are a lifeline for journalists; without them, reporters would not have access to the information they need to write stories and meet deadlines. At the same time, reporters carefully must cultivate and evaluate their sources.

Reporters and their sources have a complicated relationship. Sources may have their own agenda, and they often will attempt to use journalists to present their own point of view to the public. Reporters must understand this tendency and must test the accuracy of any information passed along by sources.

Effective Interview Techniques

Journalists depend on interviews to obtain the information necessary to write their stories. Preparing for the interview is critical; if a reporter lacks basic knowledge of his or her subject, the subject quickly will realize the reporter's lack of knowledge and will be less likely to cooperate.

Walking into an interview with a basic list of questions is a good idea. Further, be prepared to adapt or improvise if the response to a question opens a different line of inquiry. Listen carefully to each response and try to avoid thinking ahead to the next question. You may miss some important information.

Another important skill is to ask open-ended questions (e.g., questions that begin with "Why...," "How...," or "Tell me about..."). These sorts of questions allow the interviewee to give a full answer that includes their knowledge and feelings. Avoid questions that can answered with a simple "Yes" or "No".

Writing Principles

Associated Press

The Associated Press ("AP") stylebook is a reference guide for journalistic writing style and is considered the standard in the field. Editors and reporters use it as a guide for basic grammar and punctuation; they also use the AP stylebook to insure the proper principles and practices of reporting.

The AP stylebook is alphabetical and covers everything from the use of grammar and punctuation to specific styles for sportswriting and business writing. It also includes a section on media law and a bibliography of other writing reference materials.

Critical Thinking

Critical thinking can be viewed as a problem-solving skill. As such, critical thinking involves analyzing and evaluating information and then applying that information with clarity, accuracy, and consistency.

When a newspaper staff discusses story ideas, critical thinking is an important step in creating the final product readers will see. Editors and reporters must analyze ideas for their overall audience appeal. They then must determine whether they can gather sufficient relevant information for the story and formulate a plan to complete each story by that issue's deadline.

Freewriting

Journalists can use freewriting to work through writer's block. This technique involves writing for a set time about any subject as quickly as possible, without concern for transition, proper

Copyright © Mometrix Media. You have been licensed one copy of this document for personal use only. Any other reproduction or redistribution is strictly prohibited. All rights reserved.
This content is provided for test preparation purposes only and does not imply an endorsement by Mometrix of any particular political, scientific, or religious point of view.

punctuation, or grammar. While the result will lack sufficient polish for publication, it can help collect initial thoughts and ideas.

Creative writers and writing teachers use freewriting more frequently than do journalists because of the time constraints faced by the latter. Nonetheless, journalists can benefit from the exercise by using it to get in "writing mode."

Audience Segments

Segmentation is a process that divides the audience into groups based on age, gender, income, education, and other factors.

A basic knowledge of those persons who consume media helps both the editorial and advertising sides of a news operation. Editors and reporters can identify and pursue story ideas based on the age or income of a likely viewer or reader, while the same information can inform advertisers by targeting potential buyers for their products.

With different backgrounds and learning styles, high-school students reflect myriad changes in society. This diversity will influence how they use—and interact with—media, and how they develop their communication skills.

From a practical standpoint, addressing all audience segments also improves the long-term viability of a journalism product. Future readers and viewers will demand attention to the issues and events important to them.

Newsworthy Story

The most important factors in making a story newsworthy are timeliness, significance, proximity, and prominence. In a digital world, readers are accustomed to continuous news updates, so a story must be current and relevant. Readers are not interested in week-old news. A story that affects a large number of people attracts a larger audience. Events that occur near a reader's hometown (or cover a shared experience like a football game) will also prove more newsworthy. Finally, events that involve politicians, celebrities, and other people of note demand more coverage.

Eliminating Jargon

Jargon is language used by people who work in a particular field or share a common interest. While people within each specific field understand these terms, such terms often are meaningless to the typical newspaper reader.

When writing a story, journalists must consider their audience. Baseball writers do not need to write out "runs batted in," because they know their audience is aware of the abbreviation "RBI." However, including the term "rightsize" in a story about a factory closing obscures the fact that people have lost their jobs because of the closing. Journalists always should strive to write explicitly and precisely.

Clarity

Clarity attracts a reader's attention and maintains his or her interest throughout the entire article. Student reporters can develop this skill by writing with an active voice, fostering curiosity regarding the world around them, and presenting the information they gather without filters or preconceptions.

Copyright © Mometrix Media. You have been licensed one copy of this document for personal use only. Any other reproduction or redistribution is strictly prohibited. All rights reserved.
This content is provided for test preparation purposes only and does not imply an endorsement by Mometrix of any particular political, scientific, or religious point of view.

BREVITY

Consumers of printed and electronic media increasingly are pressed for time. They also have many more options for getting their news. As a result, consumers likely will ignore a poorly written story that meanders or fails to maintain its essential focus.

LEAD

The lead (also spelled "lede") comprises the first few sentences or paragraphs of a news story. A well-written lead is critical for attracting the reader's attention. It functions as the hook that will compel the reader to continue and read the entire article.

A lead should include the essential facts, with each sentence and paragraph building upon the last. The lead should avoid vague language and secondary details; instead, it should emphasize active verbs that convey energy and action.

BIAS

Bias in journalism refers to conscious (or unconscious) decisions to cover certain stories, or the manner in which journalists produce stories for publication.

As a practical matter, reporters cannot mention everything in a story. One of the skills of journalism is the ability to synthesize information; specifically, the reporter must discern between the essential facts to include and the unimportant filler omit. Journalists should seek out both sides of a news story and avoid any perception of conflict of interest, as this will undermine the standards of the profession.

EDITORIALIZING

Editorializing occurs when reporters insert their own opinions into a news story. Such opinions should be limited to the editorial section of a newspaper, and they should be labeled clearly as such.

Opinions expressed in a straight news story should be limited to quotes from sources or persons interviewed for that story. Such quotes add interest and flavor to a news article; however, reporters should be sure to include both sides of the story or issue.

CAPTIONS

Captions are short descriptions and explanations that accompany an illustration or a photograph. A good caption concisely identifies the contents of a photo or illustration. It also explains its relevance to the accompanying story.

A good caption should be easy to read and limited to a few sentences. Readability also includes selecting a type style that helps it stand apart from the text of the news article.

CATCHLINE

A catchline is an abbreviated title that appears above a photo cutline (and below the photograph). The goal of a catchline is to be creative with two or three words and attract the reader's attention.

AUDIENCES

Audiences are important to mass media because advertisers purchase time and space based on whether readers and viewers will notice their messages. Advertisers provide the bulk of revenues for newspapers, radio stations, television stations, and online websites.

Copyright © Mometrix Media. You have been licensed one copy of this document for personal use only. Any other reproduction or redistribution is strictly prohibited. All rights reserved.
This content is provided for test preparation purposes only and does not imply an endorsement by Mometrix of any particular political, scientific, or religious point of view.

Copyediting Symbols

Copyediting symbols serve as a kind of shorthand when editing a news story. In a deadline environment, a copyeditor can mark corrections quickly on a hard copy by using these symbols (e.g., a period with a circle around it means "insert period at the end of a sentence"). Reporters then can incorporate these changes into the final version of the story.

Copyright © Mometrix Media. You have been licensed one copy of this document for personal use only. Any other reproduction or redistribution is strictly prohibited. All rights reserved.
This content is provided for test preparation purposes only and does not imply an endorsement by Mometrix of any particular political, scientific, or religious point of view.

Foundations of Journalism

History of Media

John Peter Zenger and Freedom of the Press

John Peter Zenger, an 18th-century publisher and printer, was arrested in 1734, after William Cosby, the colonial governor of New York, became angry at criticisms of Cosby published in Zenger's newspaper, the New York Weekly Journal.

Zenger spent eight months in prison before his case came to trial. Noted Philadelphia lawyer Andrew Hamilton defended Zenger at his trial. Hamilton literally based his defense on the facts. Even if it could be established that Zenger's published criticisms of Cosby were defamatory, all statements within the articles were based upon established facts. In such cases, Hamilton argued, such statements could not be considered libelous. Although Governor Cosby selected the members of the jury, they agreed with Hamilton's defense and found Zenger not guilty. In doing so, the jury effectively rejected the libel laws of that era and allowed journalists to express their opinions freely.

Political Journalism

Common Sense, a 48-page manifesto written by Thomas Paine, called upon the American colonies to declare independence from Britain. This work arguably represents the earliest example of political journalism in America. Published in early 1776, Common Sense sold 500,000 copies within a year.

Democracy in America, a two-volume set written by Alexis de Tocqueville in the 1830s, still is considered a benchmark in explaining the strengths and weaknesses of American government. De Tocqueville's political analysis included his predictions that the slavery debate eventually would divide the United States.

Penny Press

The penny press was a 19th-century phenomenon that extended journalism's audience beyond the upper social classes. Typical newspapers of that era targeted the upper classes, used documents as their primary sources, and cost about six cents per issue.

In contrast, a **penny press** newspaper only cost one cent and reflected the interest of the working class with more timely news items such as court cases, police activity, and human-interest stories. Spurred by the introduction of the New York Herald in 1835, the penny press also introduced the concepts of gathering information through observation and interviews. These reporting skills soon became a journalistic standard.

The penny press also established a new financial model for newspapers. Rather than depending on subscriptions or daily sales, publishers of the penny press sold advertising space within their papers. This consistent income stream, along with the decreasing cost of paper, allowed the penny press to offer their product at a lower price. These changes in costs and income expanded the potential audience for newspapers. As happened with the new reporting skills, this new practice became a standard for the industry.

Yellow Journalism

Yellow journalism, which peaked in the 1890s, was a style of writing and presentation that distorted and exaggerated its content in order to create controversy and increase sales.

Copyright © Mometrix Media. You have been licensed one copy of this document for personal use only. Any other reproduction or redistribution is strictly prohibited. All rights reserved.
This content is provided for test preparation purposes only and does not imply an endorsement by Mometrix of any particular political, scientific, or religious point of view.

Yellow journalism had its genesis in New York City newspapers owned by Joseph Pulitzer (New York World) and William Randolph Hearst (New York Journal). Pulitzer and Hearst were engaged in a fierce circulation war. In order to lure more readers, reporters at the aforementioned papers replaced factual news stories with highly opinionated articles featuring fabricated interviews and large, misleading headlines.

While the worst excesses of yellow journalism had faded by the early 20th-century, the era serves as a reminder that promotion and sensationalism are a threat to the trust inherent in daily journalism.

Publishers who emphasized yellow journalism (such as Joseph Pulitzer and William Randolph Hearst) were obsessed with increasing the circulation of their newspapers. To attract attention, these papers emphasized large illustrations on their front pages. They also were among the first newspapers to print Sunday supplements in color. In addition, they used comic strips, games, and contests to lure more readers.

Radio

Radio was the dominant mass communication medium from the 1920s to the early 1950s. Used extensively by armed forces during World War I, radio became enormously popular following the war. By early 1922, one million radio sets were in use in the United States.

The commercial development of radio crystallized in the early 1920s, as national networks (e.g., NBC Radio, CBS Radio) established a framework of individual stations broadcasting the same shows at the same time. News became one of the mainstays of the programming mix, along with music, comedy, and drama.

Television

Television supplanted radio as the dominant mass communication medium after World War II. The NBC network introduced the first regularly scheduled television news show (The Camel Newsreel Theatre) in 1948; the 10-minute program showed newsreels from Movietone News.

In 1963, both NBC and CBS expanded their nightly news reports from 15 minutes to 30 minutes. The networks also introduced early-morning news programs such as The Today Show on NBC. By combining words with powerful images, television news extended the impact of radio and became an integral part of broadcast journalism.

Muckraking

Muckraking was a journalistic movement that emerged in the late 19th century. Muckraking reporters' goals were to expose political corruption, business fraud, and dangerous labor conditions. This investigative style of reporting led to many government reforms that addressed issues raised by muckraking journalists. One of the most notable instances of reforms spawned by muckraking occurred following publication of Upton Sinclair's The Jungle in 1906. Sinclair's unflinching description of dangerous and unhealthy conditions in the meatpacking industry led to the passage of the federal Pure Food and Drug Act later that year.

Contemporary journalism has shed light on many legal, social, and public policy issues. Recent examples include the ongoing coverage of the BP oil spill and examinations of the pace of recovery five years after Hurricane Katrina.

Investigative reporters' collective work reinforces the principle that a major responsibility of journalism involves forcing persons in power to remain honest.

Copyright © Mometrix Media. You have been licensed one copy of this document for personal use only. Any other reproduction or redistribution is strictly prohibited. All rights reserved.
This content is provided for test preparation purposes only and does not imply an endorsement by Mometrix of any particular political, scientific, or religious point of view.

Vietnam War Coverage

Due to the growth of television, the Vietnam War was the first American conflict in which uncensored war coverage was broadcast to the public. The grim, bloody images viewers saw in their living rooms each weeknight served as a direct contrast to the positive updates provided by government spokespersons.

This effect of "bringing the war home" was credited with turning American opinion against the war in the late 1960s. Perhaps the best example of the media's role in this change was Walter Cronkite's visit to Vietnam in early 1968. Cronkite, anchor of the CBS Evening News, returned from Vietnam and delivered a withering editorial commentary that the war was unwinnable.

Broadcast-News Story

A reporter must take a different approach to writing copy for a televised or radio news story than for a print story. Broadcast copy is written to be spoken; in contrast, consumers silently read print copy.

Broadcast scripts must complement the accompanying video images and audio track. A well-written paragraph will not make sense if it does not relate to the images shown on the screen. The script also must have dramatic unity, building cause and effect to a climax.

A good script should be concise and conversational in tone. Reading a broadcast story aloud serves as the best way to determine its effectiveness. As with a print story, the script also must maintain accuracy regarding fact and context.

Internet

Journalism on the internet has several advantages: capacity, flexibility, permanence, immediacy, and interactivity. Online forms of journalism can present far more information than can be shown on television. In addition, online journalism disseminates information far more quickly than can a newspaper.

Online journalism is also a medium of convergence. A variety of styles and formats can co-exist on a Web site, and it can accommodate traditional media formats (e.g., text, photographs, graphics, audio, and video).

Media Consolidation

Over the past 20 years, mass media ownership increasingly has become concentrated among a handful of companies. For example, the Disney Corporation owns ABC and ESPN, Comcast recently purchased NBC, and Time Warner owns CNN and Time magazine.

Potential problems with concentrated media ownership include the following: divided loyalties to sponsors and advertisers, less innovation and higher prices for printed and electronic content, and reduced motivation to investigate stories that might reflect badly upon the parent company.

Online Convergence

Newspaper readership has declined consistently over the past ten years. People still are interested in current events, but they are more likely to access news online via their computers or smartphones rather than read a newspaper.

Online convergence refers to the concept of posting content over a wide variety of media. Newspaper reporters may tape audio or video reports for their paper's Web site, and they may supplement their news articles with comments on a blog. Broadcast journalists may post written

Copyright © Mometrix Media. You have been licensed one copy of this document for personal use only. Any other reproduction or redistribution is strictly prohibited. All rights reserved.
This content is provided for test preparation purposes only and does not imply an endorsement by Mometrix of any particular political, scientific, or religious point of view.

material for their station's site, accompanied by the graphics and video that appeared in the original story.

Influential Media Figures

Johann Gutenberg

Johann Gutenberg (1398-1468) invented the printing press and was one of the first persons to use movable type printing. He also developed a process to mass produce movable type. Book production previously had consisted of handwritten manuscripts produced in limited supplies.

Gutenberg's innovations effectively introduced the era of mass media. As printing technology spread across Europe, news and information traveled much faster. The ability to share ideas increased literacy across the continent and foreshadowed all subsequent advancements in communication.

Benjamin Franklin

Benjamin Franklin wore many career hats throughout his life. Franklin is perhaps best known for his role in helping write the Declaration of Independence and uniting the American colonies as a nation.

However, Franklin also gained notoriety as a newspaper editor and printer in Philadelphia. By acquiring The Pennsylvania Gazette in 1729, Franklin had an outlet to publish essays and commentary regarding social issues of the day. He often contributed opinion pieces to the Gazette under assumed names.

From the time of Franklin's purchase through the early 19th century, the Gazette was one of the country's most prominent newspapers. It was considered the most successful paper in the colonies and printed the first political cartoon in America.

Frederick Douglass

Frederick Douglass (1818-1895) became a leader in the abolitionist movement in the United States. His primary contribution to journalism was as publisher of the North Star, a newspaper published from 1847 to 1851.

While still an American slave during the 1840s, Douglass left the US and spent two years living in Ireland and England. In the course of becoming a free man during that period, supporters of Douglass helped him purchase a printing press. Douglass began publishing the North Star in 1847, upon his return to Rochester, New York.

Through his writings in the North Star, Douglass advocated for the US Constitution as an anti-slavery document. The newspaper helped politicize the anti-slavery and emancipation movements; in addition, it supported women's rights.

Joseph Pulitzer

As publisher of the New York World, Joseph Pulitzer introduced two seemingly conflicting styles: new journalism and yellow journalism.

Pulitzer used the World as a vehicle to attack big business and corruption; however, he also introduced yellow journalism, a style of writing that exaggerated and fabricated stories to increase circulation.

Copyright © Mometrix Media. You have been licensed one copy of this document for personal use only. Any other reproduction or redistribution is strictly prohibited. All rights reserved.
This content is provided for test preparation purposes only and does not imply an endorsement by Mometrix of any particular political, scientific, or religious point of view.

In terms of readership, the World was an unqualified success. Circulation increased from 15,000 to 600,000 during Pulitzer's time as publisher. The World was one of the first newspapers to depend upon advertising for revenue. Pulitzer's vision of a publication that appealed to the common person ushered in the era of mass-circulation journalism.

Nellie Bly

Nellie Bly was the nom de plume of Elizabeth Jane Cochran. Frustrated by assignments to cover fashion, gardening, and other topics for the women's section of a Pittsburgh newspaper, Bly moved to New York City in 1887. After the New York World hired Bly, she accepted an undercover assignment that changed her career.

Bly checked into a boarding house and acted as if she were mentally ill. Her portrayal was so convincing that a judge had her committed to a women's asylum in the New York area. Bly witnessed the demeaning and wretched conditions inside the asylum before the World arranged to have her released.

Subsequently, Bly described her experiences in Ten Days in a Mad-House, a book that generated a grand-jury investigation, increased funding for mental health care, and established more thorough examinations for persons prior to commitment to mental institutions.

Edward R. Murrow

Edward R. Murrow (1908-1965) was one of the first journalists to move successfully from radio to television. Already well known for his reports from Europe during World War II, Murrow began his transition to television in late 1951, when his Hear It Now radio show moved to CBS Television and was renamed See It Now.

The pinnacle of Murrow's television career was a 1954 See It Now episode entitled "A Report on Senator Joseph McCarthy." McCarthy, a Wisconsin senator, was a fervent anti-Communist. Using his post as chairperson of the House Committee on Un-American Activities, McCarthy ruthlessly accused thousands of US citizens of subversion and disloyalty.

The effect of "McCarthyism" was so profound that CBS did not pay for any advance advertising of the See It Now report. When Murrow dug into his own pocket to pay for the ads, CBS did not allow him to use the company's logo. Despite the network's misgivings, Murrow's exposé of McCarthy's tactics turned public opinion against the senator. The program demonstrated the impact that investigative journalism could have in the relatively new medium of television.

Katharine Graham

Katharine Graham (1917-2001) assumed control of The Washington Post in 1963 after her husband, Philip, committed suicide. At that time, no other woman held the top position at a major American newspaper.

Graham and her editor, Benjamin Bradlee, played a major role in uncovering the Watergate scandal, the major political story of the 1970s. Bob Woodward and Carl Bernstein, then lower-level reporters at the Post, began uncovering evidence of illegal tactics employed by members of President Richard Nixon's re-election campaign.

At several critical points, Graham and Bradlee published Woodward and Bernstein's stories despite angry denials and not-so-subtle threats from the Nixon administration. Other newspapers, notably the New York Times, noticed the Post's Watergate coverage and uncovered significant evidence

Copyright © Mometrix Media. You have been licensed one copy of this document for personal use only. Any other reproduction or redistribution is strictly prohibited. All rights reserved.
This content is provided for test preparation purposes only and does not imply an endorsement by Mometrix of any particular political, scientific, or religious point of view.

over the next two years. The steady stream of investigative reporting led to Nixon resignation from the presidency in August 1974.

Barbara Walters

Barbara Walters (b. 1929) was the first female co-anchor of a national evening-news broadcast. She was also the first female co-host of The Today Show on NBC, and she spent 25 years as a correspondent for the ABC newsmagazine show, 20/20.

Walters began her career at a time when women were not taken seriously in journalism. After being hired by NBC News in the early 1960s, Walters became the "Today Girl" on The Today Show, giving the weather forecast and reporting feature stories. Such assignments were typical for female reporters, who rarely were seen and were considered incapable of reporting hard news.

Walters quickly moved up to full-reporter status on Today. In 1976, she joined Harry Reasoner as co-anchor on the ABC Evening News. In 1979, she joined 20/20 and gained a reputation for in-depth interviews of major political figures and celebrities. Her 1999 interview with Monica Lewinsky, a White House intern involved with President Bill Clinton in a sex scandal, attracted 74 million viewers, a record for a televised journalism interview.

Legal Principles in Media

First Amendment

The First Amendment of the United States Constitution states, "Congress shall make no law respecting an establishment of religion, or prohibiting the free exercise thereof, or abridging the freedom of speech, or of the press, or the right of the people peaceably to assemble, and to petition the Government for a redress of grievances."

As it relates to freedom of the press, the First Amendment prohibits any government entity (federal, state, or local) from interfering with the printing and distribution of information. Nonetheless, some limits to First Amendment press freedoms exist, such as those regarding issues of defamation law and copyright law.

Freedom of the Press

A 1938 US Supreme Court decision, Lovell v. City of Griffin, expanded the definition of press freedom. The Court ruled that the city of Griffin, Georgia, could not demand publishers of all printed materials to obtain a license from the city before distributing said materials.

The ruling, which defined the press as "every sort of publication which affords a vehicle of information and opinion," extended First Amendment protection beyond newspapers and magazines. When online blogs became common in the early 21st century, the Lovell decision provided constitutional protection for those writers, as well.

Freedom of Information Act

The Freedom of Information Act (FOIA) is a 1966 federal law that allows for the disclosure of information of US government documents. A 1996 amendment extended the law to make records available in electronic formats and provide reading rooms for such formats.

Under the FOIA, journalists make requests to obtain records of the operations and performance of the federal government. All states have their own version of the federal law (e.g., "Open Records

Copyright © Mometrix Media. You have been licensed one copy of this document for personal use only. Any other reproduction or redistribution is strictly prohibited. All rights reserved.
This content is provided for test preparation purposes only and does not imply an endorsement by Mometrix of any particular political, scientific, or religious point of view.

Act," "Right to Know Act"), and state law often covers records at the city, county, or other local levels.

The law requires a response to FOIA requests within 10 days. In reality, the actual response time is often much longer since more than 600,000 requests are made each year. Despite bureaucratic obstacles, the FOIA has allowed journalists to examine millions of documents and has compelled government to be more accessible and accountable to its citizens.

FAIR USE

Fair use is an element of US copyright law that allows limited use of material without requiring the permission of the copyright holder.

In journalism, the concept of fair use applies to issues of comment and criticism. When writing a music review, quoting a few lines from a song lyric qualifies as fair use. The same principle applies when summarizing an article from a professional journal within a news story.

Four factors are used to resolve fair use disputes:

1. Purpose and character: namely, was the material used to create something new?
2. Nature of the copyrighted work: fair use applies differently to factual works than compared to works of fiction such as plays or novels.
3. Amount of the portion taken: using several paragraphs from a short story or several stanzas of a song probably will not qualify as fair use.
4. Effect upon the potential market for the copyrighted work.

SHIELD LAWS

Shield laws protect reporters from being forced to reveal their sources to the courts or to law-enforcement officials (through subpoenas or other court orders). These laws are an extension of a basic journalism tenet—without sources providing information to reporters, many news stories never would find publication.

Shield laws currently exist in 36 of the 50 states. Depending on the statute, shield laws may apply to civil court cases but not to criminal proceedings. Shield laws also can extend to publishers, editors, and others involved with gathering and publishing information.

Reporters must not assume that a shield law will keep them out of jail. Some journalists have faced incarceration rather than name sources. One example is Judith Miller, a New York Times reporter jailed for 85 days in 2005 after refusing to disclose her sources for a story she wrote regarding leaks within the Central Intelligence Agency.

PRIOR RESTRAINT

Prior restraint is an action taken by various branches of governments to prevent release of information to the public.

Prior restraint can be exercised before a document is published, or it can be used to stop the ongoing release of documents. Often used during wartime, prior restraint can prevent military secrets from becoming public.

The judicial branch of government often exercises prior restraint with a gag order. Such an order prevents attorneys or anyone involved with the trial from commenting. It also prevents journalists from reporting any comments.

Copyright © Mometrix Media. You have been licensed one copy of this document for personal use only. Any other reproduction or redistribution is strictly prohibited. All rights reserved.
This content is provided for test preparation purposes only and does not imply an endorsement by Mometrix of any particular political, scientific, or religious point of view.

One of the best-known examples of prior restraint occurred in the 1971 Pentagon Papers case. The administration of President Richard Nixon attempted to stop the New York Times and Washington Post from publishing excerpts of a confidential government history of US involvement in the Vietnam War. The US Supreme Court overturned the government order and thus allowed the excerpts to become public record.

Absolute and Qualified Privilege

Absolute privilege applies to information acquired from court documents, police reports, and other sources considered public record. Qualified privilege can be used as a defense when a reporter is covering a trial; publishing testimony and statements made during the trial is considered part of a journalist's job.

Tinker vs. Des Moines

Tinker v. Des Moines, decided by the US Supreme Court in 1969, involved three Iowa students (two in high school, one in junior high school) who wore black armbands to protest the Vietnam War. The Des Moines school board suspended the three students and cited a policy that banned the wearing of armbands to school.

In a 7 to 2 decision, the Court held that the First Amendment right to freedom of speech and expression—guaranteed to adults—also extended to students in public high schools.

School administrators needed a valid constitutional reason to regulate or censor speech, not "a mere desire to avoid the discomfort and unpleasantness that always accompany an unpopular viewpoint."

The Tinker case established a precedent that preserves the First Amendment rights of students. School officials do not have the absolute right to cancel a story that they find objectionable.

Ginsberg v. New York

In 1968, the Supreme Court decided in Ginsberg v. New York that material not considered obscene by adult standards still could be harmful to minors.

Ginsberg, who owned a store that sold magazines on Long Island, was accused and found guilty of selling "girlie" magazine to two 16-year-old boys. The conviction rested upon on a New York state law prohibiting the sale of pictures depicting nudity to minors under age 17.

The high court rejected Ginsberg's argument that New York State could not define obscenity for one group (adults), yet apply a different definition to another group (minors under age 17). The majority opinion held that states had the power to protect minors, including barring them from purchasing magazine intended for adults.

New York Times Co. v. Sullivan

New York Times Co. v. Sullivan was a 1964 US Supreme Court decision that established the "actual malice" standard in libel cases against journalists.

Sullivan evolved from a full-page advertisement published by the Times in March 1960. The ad sought funds to defend Martin Luther King, Jr. in an Alabama perjury case and included statements regarding the actions of police officers in Montgomery, Alabama.

Copyright © Mometrix Media. You have been licensed one copy of this document for personal use only. Any other reproduction or redistribution is strictly prohibited. All rights reserved.
This content is provided for test preparation purposes only and does not imply an endorsement by Mometrix of any particular political, scientific, or religious point of view.

The public safety commissioner of Montgomery, L.B. Sullivan, claimed that the inaccurate information defamed his role as police supervisor. He demanded that the Times publish a retraction. When the newspaper rejected his demand, Sullivan filed a lawsuit.

In ruling against Sullivan, the high court held that any public figure suing for libel must prove that the allegedly harmful material was published with "actual malice." As such, the plaintiff had to demonstrate that a reporter or news organization knew the published material was untrue or published the material in reckless disregard for the truth.

The Sullivan decision established a high burden of proof. Furthermore, as a result of this suit, it is virtually impossible for public figures or public officials to prevail in a libel suit against the media.

Hazelwood School District v. Kuhlmeier

Hazelwood School District v. Kuhlmeier originated with articles written for the student newspaper of Hazelwood East High School near St. Louis, Missouri. The principal of Hazelwood East High School reviewed each issue of the paper prior to publication, and upon review the principal removed articles scheduled to appear in the paper.

The Supreme Court based its ruling—a reversal of a federal appeals-court decision—on a finding that the student newspaper was a not a "forum for public expression." By so doing, the Court opened the door for censorship if a school could provide a pedagogical (educational) reason for deleting a story.

The Hazelwood case represents a further interpretation of Tinker v. Des Moines, which established that students did not check their First Amendment rights at the schoolhouse door. Their rights to freedom of speech and expression extended to the classroom.

Hazelwood amended that guarantee by giving administrators more control over school-sponsored publications. Nonetheless, any decision to censor stories must have a "legitimate pedagogical concern." School officials do not have the absolute right to cancel a story they find objectionable.

Since the Hazelwood ruling, some states have passed laws granting greater First Amendment protection to student newspapers. In addition, the decision does not affect publications produced by students in private schools.

Ethical Principles in Media

Credibility

Credibility addresses the basic trust between journalists and their respective audiences. Readers must have confidence that reported materials are objective and factual.

As stated in the Preamble to the Code of Ethics for the Society of Professional Journalists, "The duty of the journalist is to...seek truth and [provide] a fair and comprehensive account of events and issues. Professional integrity is the cornerstone of a journalist's credibility."

Attribution

Attribution indicates the source of information in a news article. Clearly indicating which person provided certain information is essential to writing a credible story.

When a journalist includes information that does not come from his or her own firsthand observation, he or she should always employ attribution. The journalist always should include the

Copyright © Mometrix Media. You have been licensed one copy of this document for personal use only. Any other reproduction or redistribution is strictly prohibited. All rights reserved.
This content is provided for test preparation purposes only and does not imply an endorsement by Mometrix of any particular political, scientific, or religious point of view.

source's full name; if important to the story, the source's job title should appear as well. Journalists can use both paraphrased information and direct quotes from attributed sources.

Obscenity

Legally, "obscenity" refers to words or images that the average person (applying contemporary community standards) would find offensive and lacking in literary or artistic values.

Obscene material can become minefield for student journalists. A reporter might consider something humorous or "cutting-edge, while readers, parents, and/or school officials might consider the same material obscene. The consequences for publishing legally offensive material can range from cancellation of future issues to possible further legal action.

Faculty advisors, in cooperation with school administrators and the student staff, should adopt an anti-obscenity policy. In addition to the legal definition, student journalists also should be aware of obscenity laws at the local level.

Libel

Libel is an action that causes personal or professional harm to an individual's reputation. Most libel cases result from published reports of scandals and crimes.

Accurate reporting of a libelous claim does not prevent a journalist from being sued for libel. The best defense in such cases is that the statement in question is "provably true;" the journalist then can defend the report under either absolute or qualified privilege.

Plagiarism

Plagiarism is defined as using the language, thoughts, and ideas of another author without proper credit. The key to recognizing plagiarism lies in knowing the difference between information considered common knowledge versus original ideas put forth by other writers.

Poor handling of sources can be confused with plagiarism. Journalism instructors should emphasize correct procedures for quoting, paraphrasing, and citation.

Using a complete sentence or significant phrase verbatim and without credit constitutes cut-and-paste plagiarism. Writers should set off such content with quotation marks and identify the source. Lifting complete paragraphs and merely switching around a few words also constitutes plagiarism.

Conflict of Interest

A conflict of interest occurs when a reporter or editor has a connection to a story or issue that might influence how they write and cover the story.

Some conflicts of interest are obvious (e.g., a reporter who owns stock in a company and covers the company as part of the business beat). However, conflicts also can arise from personal relationships or off-work activities. For example, most news organizations ban journalists from political involvement.

In cases of unavoidable conflict, journalists should disclose them in order to avoid bias and protect their credibility.

Ethical Manipulation of Images

A photograph that incorporates special techniques to enhance the presentation of a fireworks display is considered an ethical manipulation, provided the graphic is marked clearly as a photo-

Copyright © Mometrix Media. You have been licensed one copy of this document for personal use only. Any other reproduction or redistribution is strictly prohibited. All rights reserved.
This content is provided for test preparation purposes only and does not imply an endorsement by Mometrix of any particular political, scientific, or religious point of view.

illustration. Other permissible special techniques include the use of a telephoto lens or fish-eye lens for photographs.

Unethical Manipulation of Images

Digitally altering a photo by removing and/or adding elements to the original (e.g., photoshopping) is considered unethical if the changes are not noted in the caption/cutline.

Internet

Copy and graphics posted on the Internet are considered published material; therefore, they are not considered in the public domain (e.g., usable by anyone without proper credit).

Whenever possible, journalists should use only material originally sourced by the reporter. The re-use of information accessed online must conform to US copyright law. These laws protect writers, photographers, and artists from having their works used without permission.

Role of Mass Media in Society

Mass Media

Mass communications informs its audience; in addition, it persuades, entertains, and transmits culture. It plays an important role in establishing and reflecting public opinion. Journalism instructors show students how to evaluate the messages of mass media with objectivity, analyze the method of presentation, and understand the content from different perspectives.

These skills allow students to become critical and informed media consumers. Such skills also help students recognize full and fair media coverage, the importance of ethical principles and legal guidelines, and how different types of media can shape or distort the overall message.

Journalism

Mass media is designed to reach a wide audience. The earliest mass media materials consisted of printed matter (books, manuscripts) and evolved in the early 20th century with newspapers, magazines, and national radio networks.

In many cases, electronic media supplanted printed media in the late 20th century. The emergence of online technologies has enabled journalists to extend their reach beyond the local newspaper or television station. However, online expansion also has commoditized the news. Consumers can obtain information from any number of online sources; in most cases, consumers' only cost is the monthly charge for an Internet or wireless connection.

Free Press

The First Amendment of the US Constitution grants broad rights to journalists: "Congress shall make no law...abridging freedom of the press." This statement protects the press from interference from all levels of government: state, local, and federal.

At the same time, many media consumers believe that a free, independent press must also regulate itself. This includes making print and electronic journalism more open and accountable to public scrutiny.

While newspapers quickly report errors, they rarely take the time to examine the overall quality of their work. Public perception of the media has declined over time; readers and viewers tend to judge the quality and credibility of journalism by its least responsible members.

Copyright © Mometrix Media. You have been licensed one copy of this document for personal use only. Any other reproduction or redistribution is strictly prohibited. All rights reserved.
This content is provided for test preparation purposes only and does not imply an endorsement by Mometrix of any particular political, scientific, or religious point of view.

Tabloids

The emergence of the Internet since 2000 has generated a round-the-clock interest in sensational stories. Websites such as the Drudge Report (news), TMZ.com (celebrities) and Deadspin.com (sports) are often the first outlets to report the misbehavior of politicians, movie stars, and sports figures.

Newspaper editors and television news producers cannot ignore the interest of their respective audiences. As a result, coverage of celebrities and popular culture has increased to match the increased level of interest.

Tabloid Journalism

"Tabloid journalism" is a catchall phrase for publications that emphasize coverage of celebrities and popular culture.

In print media, tabloid journalism is known best for weekly newspapers such as the National Enquirer and magazines such as People and Us Weekly that are sold at supermarket check stands.

In electronic media, the success of Entertainment Tonight (ET) in the 1980s demonstrated the increased demand for news regarding the personal lives of celebrities. Often broadcast following the local news, ET attracted a loyal following and commanded higher advertising rates than other shows in similar time slots.

Entertainment

Entertainment encompasses movies, music, and sports. The evolution of video games has expanded that definition, and consumers now can access more entertainment options from more sources than at any other time in history.

In the past, people had to go to a theatre in order to view a motion picture. Now people can experience the same motion picture at home on a DVD player, online from the local cable company, or on an iPhone or similar device.

Advocacy

The mass media (which now includes online sources such as blogs, videos, and podcasts) can advocate for business concerns or social issues.

The goal of social-issue advocacy is to influence public policy. Examples include ads to help elect political candidates or campaigns to improve health and safety. On the business side, companies use advertising to increase awareness and sales of specific products, and then they often employ marketing and public relations campaigns to improve the public perception of a given product or industry.

Public-Service Advertising

Public-service advertising raises awareness of a social issue, humanitarian cause, or religious viewpoint. This type of advertising differs from display or classified advertising, both which focus on marketing or selling a specific product.

Usually a non-profit organization such as the United Way, the Red Cross, or another civic group sponsors public-service advertising. In most cases, the newspaper donates the cost of this space. These ads can prove useful when a newspaper's add sales are insufficient to fill all of the advertising space in an issue.

Copyright © Mometrix Media. You have been licensed one copy of this document for personal use only. Any other reproduction or redistribution is strictly prohibited. All rights reserved.
This content is provided for test preparation purposes only and does not imply an endorsement by Mometrix of any particular political, scientific, or religious point of view.

Classified Advertising

Unlike display advertising, classified advertising is predominantly text-based. Classified ads usually appear in their own section, separate from the editorial content. Display advertising literally is "displayed" next to news stories on the editorial side.

Classified advertising allows private parties to buy, sell, or rent items. The ads can be as simple as listing the type of item for sale, a price, and a contact number. Furthermore, classified ads often are grouped within categories (e.g., Automobiles, Apartments for Rent).

Broadcast Journalism

Staff Roles During a Broadcast News Program

The audio technician is the sound version of the technical director, controlling the microphones, audio tape, and music for televised news program. The audio technician selects the various audio elements through a mixing board.

The graphics operator creates on-screen titles and graphics to appear on screen, and this person is responsible for the accuracy of these graphics and titles. Production assistants operate the teleprompters and set up the rigging (pulleys and cables) that position the lighting on the news set.

Station Manager

Whether managing a radio station or a television station, station managers are responsible for day-to-day operations. These responsibilities include scheduling the on-air staff, scheduling the off-air staff, supervising promotion and advertising for the station, and assuring that the station complies with federal broadcast regulation.

Station managers manage contract issues with the on-air staff, and at larger stations, they oversee the training of department managers. They also contract with outside vendors to repair or replace damaged or outdated equipment.

Television News Producer

Television news producers work much like journalists; they identify story ideas, research those stories, and then report their findings. However, a producer has the additional job of mixing images with words. This task requires the skill to present a story visually and work with a team of writers and reporters.

The producer also needs basic technical knowledge and understanding of how those aspects of a news story fit together (e.g., writing a script that matches the video images).

News Director

The news director is responsible for the overall production of the broadcast. This includes camera assignments, the positions of the news anchor and the reporters on the set, and selecting the camera shots and recorded elements used during the program.

Technical Director

The technical director controls and mixes the video and audio elements of a televised news program. Video elements include camera shots within the studio, stories taped in advance, and live reports from the field.

Copyright © Mometrix Media. You have been licensed one copy of this document for personal use only. Any other reproduction or redistribution is strictly prohibited. All rights reserved.
This content is provided for test preparation purposes only and does not imply an endorsement by Mometrix of any particular political, scientific, or religious point of view.

Then the technical director uses video and audio switches to select these video elements as well as audio tracks. The switchers select the specific tracks and video shots in the order they will appear on the broadcast.

(Note: In smaller television markets, the same person often acts as the news director and the technical director.)

Script Writing

Broadcast journalism employs words in concert with moving images, while print journalism depends almost totally on words. An effective broadcast script must complement the images on the screen and defer to those images when necessary.

In addition, the script must be brief. Electronic news segments have specific predetermined lengths, usually no more than a few minutes. A script that meanders or is too wordy will not match the pictures and may be too long to fit into the time slot.

Zoom Lens

The zoom lens moves the camera operator's point of view either closer to the subject or further away from the subject. The operator can adjust the zoom feature manually or by pushing a button to move the lens in and out.

The focus ring is located at the front of the lens housing. Turning the focus ring clockwise produces a closer focus, while turning the focus ring counter-clockwise produces a more distant focus.

The iris (also known as the aperture) is an adjustable opening that controls the amount of light allowed into the lens. The iris ring is usually placed around the ring housing.

White balance determines how each color appears in the frame by comparing it to a "true white" reference. A button on the video camera measures the available light to determine if the colors will render correctly.

Focusing a Video Camera Lens

The best way to focus a video camera involves the following steps: zoom in as close as possible to the subject, adjust the focus ring until the subject is in sharp focus, then zoom out to the required framing. Keep in mind that as the lens zooms in, keeping the picture steady will become more difficult.

Measuring White Balance

To measure white balance with a video camera, point the lens at a non-reflective white surface with the same amount of light as the subject. Set the focus and exposure, and then press the white balance button. On most video cameras, an indicator within the viewfinder will indicate that the proper white balance has been achieved.

External Microphone

Built-in microphones are common with consumer video cameras; however, most newsgathering tasks require an external microphone for interviews and reporter stand-ups, since the microphone often needs to be in a different place than the camera (for example, when covering a speech or a press conference).

Copyright © Mometrix Media. You have been licensed one copy of this document for personal use only. Any other reproduction or redistribution is strictly prohibited. All rights reserved.
This content is provided for test preparation purposes only and does not imply an endorsement by Mometrix of any particular political, scientific, or religious point of view.

In addition, external microphones are more sensitive and can record higher-quality sound. These characteristics are important especially for a video news segment, since poorly recorded audio will reduce a news story's impact.

Audio Levels

The audio level is the volume at which a video segment's soundtrack is recorded. Most video cameras include an "auto-gain control" that automatically adjusts sound level to the proper volume. The level also can be controlled manually.

Background and ambient noise, especially wind noise, can disrupt an audio track. The ambient-noise level should remain consistent throughout the news story. Wind noise can be diminished by using a low-cut filter control on the camera or by placing a windsock (fabric cover) over the microphone.

Cutaway Shot

A cutaway shot is a video technique that quickly switches from one image to another. Among other examples, a cutaway can show audience reaction to a football game (then cut back to action on the field) or a rock concert (cutting to images of fans shouting and applauding, then switching to a close-up of the band's lead singer).

Transition

A transition shot assures a smooth segue between stories. An example of a transition is to fade or "dissolve" from one on-screen image to the next. The effect is not jarring, but it offers enough of a visual change for the viewer to understand that a new segment is about to begin.

Voiceover

A voiceover is the technique of reading audio commentary to accompany video images. An effective voiceover must include a concise script and an audio presentation that is not "rushed." In addition, the audio track must match what appears on the screen.

CD-ROM

Hypermedia or multimedia authoring software can produce a visually interesting and easy to use CD-ROM. In each case, the software connects the print and electronic elements of the disc. Links can be included to take the user from graphics to video, from plain text to audio, and so forth.

Time Constraints in Print vs. Broadcast Journalism

Simply put, print reporters lack time and space; broadcast reporters lack time and time.

Deadlines exist in print journalism because presses must begin printing the paper at a specific time. Because delaying a press run is costly and inefficient, all stories must be written and edited prior to printing. The amount of space assigned to a story also requires the reporter to determine what to include in a story (and what to leave out).

Deadlines are even more arbitrary in broadcast journalism. A news program cannot begin 15 minutes late, since such a delay would affect the start time for all subsequent programming. A reporter in the field often must go with the facts they have at the start of the broadcast, since there is not sufficient time to obtain additional information.

Copyright © Mometrix Media. You have been licensed one copy of this document for personal use only. Any other reproduction or redistribution is strictly prohibited. All rights reserved.
This content is provided for test preparation purposes only and does not imply an endorsement by Mometrix of any particular political, scientific, or religious point of view.

Advising, Instruction, and Assessment

Teaching Journalism

Skills Necessary for Journalism Teachers

Teaching journalism at the high-school level requires a broad knowledge of several subjects. Among other skills, teachers must have a background that includes writing, media design and production, and press law and ethics. Listening skills and leadership skills also are essential. Journalism instructors often take a lead role in helping develop publications for a student audience.

Teaching High School Journalism

Journalism teachers should design a curriculum that centers on the student and has a collaborative element. Lesson plans should cover the different forms of journalistic writing (hard news, feature stories, editorials). Presentation of photos and graphics also should constitute a prominent part of the curriculum. An audience accustomed to high-quality interactive media will demand a similar level of quality from student journalists.

Learning Theory

In a journalism classroom, students should learn both individually and as a group. Creative collaboration is essential for students, especially for those students who might one day move into a career in the media. Teachers should integrate a variety of media—print, electronic, and online—into the curriculum.

The rise of the Internet (over the past decade) and social networking (in the past few years) demonstrates the rapid pace of change in communication. Teachers should integrate these changes into journalism curriculum, and they should be mindful of the further evolution of online media.

Creating an Active Classroom

Teachers should pose questions to help students articulate their ideas, promote risk-taking and problem solving, and help students question issues on their own. The instructor also should help students understand their unique role as gatekeepers of information, and discover how their own consumption of media shapes their worldview.

Evaluating Student Progress

Assessment tools include objective quizzes and tests, short-term and long-term story assignments, collaborative projects, and publications developed during the school year (e.g., issues of the student newspaper, yearbooks).

Promoting Collaborative Effort

Student journalists are still learning their craft, so the finished product often may contain copy and design errors (e.g., misspelled words and other typographical errors such as inconsistent internal margins and missing captions).

In order to keep track of the production process and assure that students spot and correct their errors prior to publication, they can be encouraged to create a checklist for editing and proofreading pages. Such a checklist could be based upon previous errors and other issues that might arise.

Copyright © Mometrix Media. You have been licensed one copy of this document for personal use only. Any other reproduction or redistribution is strictly prohibited. All rights reserved.
This content is provided for test preparation purposes only and does not imply an endorsement by Mometrix of any particular political, scientific, or religious point of view.

As students gain more experience through the school year, they can revise and expand the checklist at the pre-production and post-production stages. By creating a checklist and allowing students to add their own input, the entire staff actively is involved in continually improving the publication.

Student Publication Advisor

Serving as the faculty advisor for a student newspaper is the ultimate hands-on job. Advisors work side-by-side with student staff members to produce newspapers and other student publications.

An advisor is responsible for the editorial, business, advertising, and production of a publication. While these jobs usually are separate positions at a commercial newspaper, the advisor ultimately is responsible for all these tasks for a student newspaper.

Even though an advisor may not have any formal journalism training, he or she needs adequate knowledge of desktop publishing, publication design and layout, directing and managing a staff, and newspaper law and ethics.

Determining News Coverage and Concepts

The staff of a school publication has a unique position. As such, staff members make up part of a community tightly defined by the school campus and activities related to the campus.

Observing the reaction of students on campus provides an excellent way to determine the events that deserve coverage in a student newspaper. An awareness of students' media consumption habits also is helpful. A story communicated by photos and brief blocks of copy is more effective than a page filled with text.

Developing Journalists

An advisor helps students make sound decisions that reflect well on their newspaper and their school. As a result, the advisor should give the staff all the responsibility they can handle. If they occasionally make poor choices, the advisor can help them recognize the consequences of those choices.

Advisors should foster students' curiosity about the world around them. This includes paying attention to news events and the manner in media sources report and cover such events.

Student journalists also should read widely in order to gain exposure to various examples of good writing. They also should strive constantly to sharpen their own writing skills both inside and outside of the newsroom, since writing is the most important skill a journalist can develop.

Journalist Skills

Student journalists should be able to use language correctly and follow the rules of grammar, punctuation, and spelling. They also must maintain accuracy and pay attention to detail. This attention involves checking the spelling of every name used in a story and wording direct quotations with precision.

In addition, a good reporter must possess skepticism. He or she should question sources for possible motives or agendas, and the reporter should verify information by comparing it with other information he or she has gathered and received.

Copyright © Mometrix Media. You have been licensed one copy of this document for personal use only. Any other reproduction or redistribution is strictly prohibited. All rights reserved.
This content is provided for test preparation purposes only and does not imply an endorsement by Mometrix of any particular political, scientific, or religious point of view.

Censorship

Censorship is the suppression of any communication considered objectionable. In student journalism, a faculty advisor or member of the school administration usually reviews all content prior to publication.

Student editors and reporters often encounter obstacles when they attempt to write stories regarding controversial subjects (e.g., teen pregnancy or alcohol and drug use by students). US Supreme Court decisions such as Tinker v. Des Moines and Hazelwood v. Kuhlmeier have established precedents regarding what school administrators can and cannot do when censoring a student publication.

Student Publications

Student Yearbook Sections

Most student yearbooks have sections including individual photographs of students organized by their class year (e.g., freshmen, sophomores, juniors, seniors). Other sections chronicle boys' and girls' sports teams, activities of clubs and student organizations, and individual photos of faculty members.

Other sections may include a memorial page (for students or teachers who have died during the school year), an advertising section (which can include paid ads from parents or family members who wish to congratulate a graduating senior), and an index with a listing of the name of each person appearing in the yearbook.

School Newspaper Production

Student newspapers often tackle controversial subjects (e.g., teen pregnancy, underage drinking, etc.) that may present problems for school administrators. During the planning stages, the faculty advisor should suggest a meeting between the newspaper staff and—in most cases—the school principal.

Such a meeting provides an opportunity for the staff to explain subject matter and content for the proposed story, as well as the manner in which the newspaper will present the finished story. This collaborative approach gives the principal an opportunity to express any concerns (legal or otherwise) and address any concerns or conflicts that may arise.

By providing such advice at an early stage, the faculty advisor likely can prevent any issues that might cause a story to be pulled from the paper.

Newspaper Format vs. Yearbook Format

A student newspaper, published several times during the school year, includes the most recent events occurring in and around the school. In addition, most newspapers are divided into the front page, an inside-news section, an editorial page, and a sports section. The newspaper has a sense of immediacy and is published on newsprint.

In contrast, a yearbook offers a comprehensive look back at school activities from the entire school year. Sections include student life, sports teams, club activities, photos of faculty members, and a photo section of each class. The yearbook is intended as a long-term keepsake. It likely is printed on glossy paper (for better reproduction of the photographs) with a hardback binding.

Copyright © Mometrix Media. You have been licensed one copy of this document for personal use only. Any other reproduction or redistribution is strictly prohibited. All rights reserved.
This content is provided for test preparation purposes only and does not imply an endorsement by Mometrix of any particular political, scientific, or religious point of view.

Connecting with Target Audience

The readers of a student newspaper have grown up in a world of digital images and a 24-hour news cycle. Subsequently, the static, black-and-white style of newspapers from previous generations will not hold the attention of new generations.

Within reasonable budget limitations, student publications should emphasize color, sophisticated graphics, and dynamic photographs. The total information package should be visually interesting in order to attract the reader's attention and maintain it throughout the publication.

Student Literary Magazine

Rather than text and headlines, the cover of a student literary magazine might be devoted to a single photo or a specific piece of art. Desktop publishing software can enhance the cover and attract readers. For example, photos of a gallery of student artwork can be combined with graphics, titles, and subtitles.

A literary magazine's writing focus also differs from the focus of a student newspaper. Unlike the objective, "just the facts" approach of journalism, a literary magazine emphasizes creative writing, fiction, and poetry.

Interactive CD-ROM

High-school students, the most common audience for student yearbooks, are familiar with social networks, texting, and other forms of interactive media. A CD-ROM is a good match for this audience because the disc can include video clips, digital images, music, and information from other electronic sources.

Organizational Behavior

An organization is a group of two or more individuals working toward a set of shared goals in a manner that is coordinated, methodical and ongoing. Organizations can serve a primarily social-cultural purpose, such as schools, museums, churches; a primarily economic purpose, such as manufacturing and service industries, retailers, and banks; or exist in order to maintain order within a larger social grouping, such as military, government and police organizations. Because organizations are composed of human beings, these organizational types have considerable overlap. For example, a school adheres to schedules both within its own field of reference (staggered lunch periods and managing hallway travel are two instances), as well as outside its own needs (school holidays coincide with bank and business holidays). A hospital is both a business that schedules staff, negotiates salaries, and markets its product, as well as a community organization offering community education programs.

Editor's Role

The editor of a student newspaper likely will have spent at least one year on the staff. Accordingly, previous experience as a reporter, photographer, and/or copyeditor is helpful.

Student editors should have a good grasp of leadership, collaborative, and interpersonal skills. They also must have an excellent command of the language. If reporters file stories with incorrect language or style, then editors must recognize and be willing to change the material or demand that the reporter change it.

A broad base of knowledge is essential for an editor; it allows him or her to put events in perspective. A good editor must love the language and know how to use it.

Copyright © Mometrix Media. You have been licensed one copy of this document for personal use only. Any other reproduction or redistribution is strictly prohibited. All rights reserved.
This content is provided for test preparation purposes only and does not imply an endorsement by Mometrix of any particular political, scientific, or religious point of view.

Editors and Reporters

The relationship between editors and reporters can be confrontational.

Editors must give reporters sufficient freedom to do their jobs and exercise their best judgment regarding stories they choose and the manner in which they write their stories. At the same time, an editor must maintain the publication's standards. Editors have the final say regarding how the publication appears to the public.

Copy Editor

The copy editor has several responsibilities at a newspaper. These responsibilities include ensuring that all spelling, punctuation, and grammar are accurate and that the writing maintains a consistent style (for journalism, this means Associated Press, or "AP," style).

Copy editors also may shorten a news article to fit within a certain space. Another responsibility of the copyeditor involves correcting and eliminating any jargon in the story. Other duties include writing headlines and captions, clarifying unclear or unsubstantiated statements, and addressing any potential legal issues.

Convincing Editorial

As with other forms of writing, organizing one's thoughts and ideas is an essential first step in creating a good editorial. A journalism teacher should assist the student in developing an outline to help organize the editorial's main ideas.

An outline will help address the difficulty students may experience interpreting the context of an editorial assignment. This active, hands-on approach can be tailored to each individual student, helping him or her clearly express his or her thoughts in writing and produce an effective, convincing editorial piece.

To promote fairness and sensitivity, photojournalists should avoid creating images that reinforce stereotypes. The visual reporting of events in an ethnically diverse community should reflect the diverse beliefs of the entire community.

Factors That Affect Media Coverage

Students must be mindful of how business decisions affect media coverage and how online content has changed the role of journalism in contemporary society.

Material obtained online also raises questions regarding accuracy, legitimacy, and copyright issues. The mere fact that content appears online does not mean it is in the public domain and can be used without permission.

Advertising Revenue

Advertising comprises the primary revenue stream for any student publication. However, it may be most critical to the financial success of a yearbook.

Unlike the student newspaper (which may be published as often as once a week), the yearbook comes out only once a year. Production costs are much higher for the yearbook than for the student newspaper. Among other factors, the yearbook likely will feature a hard cover, four-color photographs, and over 200 pages.

Without sufficient advertising revenue, yearbook sales proceeds may not cover the production costs. This deficit could adversely affect the budget in subsequent school years.

Copyright © Mometrix Media. You have been licensed one copy of this document for personal use only. Any other reproduction or redistribution is strictly prohibited. All rights reserved.
This content is provided for test preparation purposes only and does not imply an endorsement by Mometrix of any particular political, scientific, or religious point of view.

Maximizing Ad Sales

An excellent way for students to learn how to sell advertising is to tap into the talents of community professionals. Advisors could invite advertising managers for local publishers to give presentations to the yearbook staff. These managers could teach sales strategies and serve as mentors for the staff. Through this interaction, students will learn to identify local firms likely to purchase a yearbook ad as well as "real world" lessons that can enhance overall advertising sales.

Students and faculty members (albeit to a lesser extent) make up the target audience for an annual yearbook. As readers scan through the publication, they will seek out activities in which they and their friends/colleagues were involved.

Yearbook advertising is usually concentrated in one section of the publication. A unique advertising layout that includes editorial content will attract attention and keep readers from skipping over the ads. One effective strategy is to surround the advertisements with candid portraits of students, coaches, and faculty members. This layout strategy will attract the reader's eye and increase chances that the reader will look at the ads, rather than skipping over them.

Advertising Deadlines

The amount of advertising in a student newspaper determines the amount of space available for editorial copy and images. Because of this, staggering advertising and editorial deadlines (with the advertising deadline set well before the editorial deadline) makes sense.

With all advertising sold and designed ahead of time, the editor can review the page layout for that issue and determine the number of stories and photos needed to fill the editorial space.

Paper Type and Quality

Newsprint is the most cost-effective solution for a student newspaper. Compared to other publications, the newspaper is printed more often and includes more copies with each issue.

Thicker, glossier papers can be considered for literary magazines and student yearbooks. The printing cost per copy for these papers is higher than the printing cost for newsprint copies, but the tradeoff for higher costs results in better reproduction of photographs and graphics. This tradeoff proves important, because most people purchasing a literary magazine or yearbook consider it a keepsake.

Cost

Factors that affect publication costs include the number of pages per issue, page size, the number of colors used for printing, the number of copies per press run, and (for a literary magazine or yearbook) the type of binding used.

Selecting a common paper size and delivering a product to the printer without last-minute revisions helps control overall costs. Also, keep in mind that four-color printing is far more costly than two-color or black-and-white printing.

Subscriptions

The subscription model is common in journalism. Subscriptions require customers to pay an upfront cost for access to a newspaper or magazine over a specific time (e.g., one year). This assures a consistent revenue stream rather than depending on single-copy sales, which can vary from issue to issue. Subscriptions also allow customers to have a publication delivered on a regular basis (daily or monthly).

Copyright © Mometrix Media. You have been licensed one copy of this document for personal use only. Any other reproduction or redistribution is strictly prohibited. All rights reserved.
This content is provided for test preparation purposes only and does not imply an endorsement by Mometrix of any particular political, scientific, or religious point of view.

Desktop Publishing

Desktop Publishing Software

Desktop publishing software utilizes a personal computer to create page layouts for publications. Learning to use desktop software is a skill student journalists need in order to pursue a career in the field.

The most popular software includes Adobe InDesign (originally Adobe PageMaker), QuarkXpress, and Microsoft Publisher. All of this software is compatible with the Windows personal-computer system.

For Macintosh users, iStudio Publisher is the most common desktop publishing software.

Vocabulary of Desktop Publishing

Alignment means lining up the top, bottom, sides, and middle of the text or graphic elements on a page.

A **bleed allowance** allows for deviations in cutting paper for the finished product; this allowance usually extends about 1/8 inch beyond the trim lines.

A **gatefold** brings the left and right edges of a page inward (with parallel folds) and meets in the middle of the page without overlapping.

Zoom Tool

The zoom tool changes the magnification of pages within a document. The page can be brought in closer for detailed work, then "zoomed out" again to view the entire page.

A magnifying glass graphic in the toolbar represents the zoom tool for desktop publishing software usually.

Web Design

Web design is the process of creating one or more pages to appear within a web browser. Each page's design should complement the site's overall appearance of the site.

Elements of Web design include graphics, color and font selection, navigation design, and content creation.

PDF File

PDF (Portable Document Format) is a file format that allows for document creation, editing, and manipulation. Adobe Acrobat is the best-known computer program for creating, editing, and manipulating PDF files. These files are viewable on any computer system with software capable of reading the files (e.g., Adobe Acrobat Reader).

PDFs can be used to publish electronic versions of printed documents and create files with links and bookmarks that are sharable via email or the Web.

Point Size and Column Width

The right typography helps make a publication more readable and legible. The size of type used for body copy should be between 9 points and 14 points, with leading 2 points more than the point size of the type (e.g., 10-point type, 12-point leading). Column widths should range from 40 to 50 characters.

Copyright © Mometrix Media. You have been licensed one copy of this document for personal use only. Any other reproduction or redistribution is strictly prohibited. All rights reserved.
This content is provided for test preparation purposes only and does not imply an endorsement by Mometrix of any particular political, scientific, or religious point of view.

Newspaper Typography

The best approach for newspaper typography is to pick two typefaces (three at the most) and stick with them. Newspapers exist for reading, not for glancing. Using too many different typefaces makes it difficult for a reader to focus on a specific story.

Reverse Type

Reverse type involves placing type on a dark background. The type is usually white against a black background. In order for the type to stand out easily on the page, it should be significantly lighter than the background.

Reverse type can call attention to a headline or sub-headline well, but it is best used sparingly.

Jump Line

The jump line identifies a story that continues on another page. The "jump" refers to the portion of the story that appears on the second page.

Modular Page Design

Modular page design can save time when creating either a printed or an electronic version of a student newspaper. In modular design, a basic template is created in which elements such as the sidebar and bottom of the page are repeated throughout the publication. Then each page's center content can be changed easily.

Screen Use

When using images placed behind a block of text, the type size of the text should be set larger than the surrounding text. The screen should be set at 5 to 10 percent; this will allow the darker text to stand out from the background image.

An inexpensive way to add contrast to a page is to use screened images, reverses, and two-color printing instead of four-color. This can save up to 40 percent in overall printing costs.

Continuity means using graphic devices (white space, images, and layout) to help readers understand the content and direct them through the material.

Signature

A signature is an expression of page counts for a magazine. A typical magazine signature has 16 pages, because the typical web offset press can print 16 pages on one sheet of paper (8 pages per side).

Each signature is folded, inserted and bound with the other signatures. A magazine with four signatures will have 64 pages, in addition to the cover.

Gutter

The gutter is the crease that appears between two facing pages of a newspaper. Text and photos (when possible) should not extend across a gutter. This makes copy difficult to read and disrupts the overall structure and flow of the page design.

Flag

The flag is the name of the newspaper that appears at the top of the page. It should be distinctive and distinguish the publication from its competition. The type font of a flag usually differs from the type used elsewhere in the publication.

Copyright © Mometrix Media. You have been licensed one copy of this document for personal use only. Any other reproduction or redistribution is strictly prohibited. All rights reserved.
This content is provided for test preparation purposes only and does not imply an endorsement by Mometrix of any particular political, scientific, or religious point of view.

Dummying

A "dummy" is a simulated version of a newspaper. Also known as a mockup, the dummy shows where the copy, photographs, and advertising will appear on each page. The dummy also indicates the amount of room available for editorial and advertising content. Since advertising space on each page is fixed, copy and photographs must be sized and/or reduced in order to fit in the remaining space.

Hard Copy Proof

A hard-copy proof allows the editor and staff physically to "see" how an entire publication will appear, from the first page to the last page. Editors and advisors, alike, are more likely to notice typographical errors as well as issues with layout and positioning on a hard-copy proof than on a computer screen.

It is also a good idea for different members of the student staff (not just the copy editor) to proof pages. This provides hands-on proofing experience for reporters and photographers and gives them a sense of how good design enhances a newspaper.

Graphics and Design

Effective Page Design

While digital imaging and desktop technology has made it easier to produce and design student publications, the traditional criteria for layout and typography still apply. An effective, well-designed page attracts the reader's eye through the prominent placement of dominant elements within the page.

The overall presentation should reinforce and enhance the written message. From a graphics perspective, the page should be easy to read, with advertising presented in a manner that does not detract from the editorial content.

Design Characteristics

Each page of a newspaper needs a dominant piece of art; most readers are attracted to a page by a strong photo or graphic. If color is included, use it to move the reader's eyes around the page or around a news package. The best use of color is for photographs and other images; colored headlines or text copy is distracting.

Logical Placement of Elements

Balance refers to the concept of placing elements on a page in order to distribute text and graphic elements evenly. As such, a page can achieve balance with multiple columns to organize text, photos, and graphics into smaller blocks of information. Contrast is the visual difference between two separate images. A clear contrast between graphics, text, and headlines creates logic and clarity in the overall design. Good design clarifies and supports the content.

Variety, Dominance, and Continuity

Variety means providing white space and other visual "rest stops" in the overall design. Pullout quotes (quotes set in larger type that paraphrase or summarize the content of the main story) help provide variety. Sidebars and related stories can add interest, as well.

Dominance refers to the use of elements with visual weight, intensity, and focus. Bold typefaces and graphics help create a focus for each page.

Copyright © Mometrix Media. You have been licensed one copy of this document for personal use only. Any other reproduction or redistribution is strictly prohibited. All rights reserved.
This content is provided for test preparation purposes only and does not imply an endorsement by Mometrix of any particular political, scientific, or religious point of view.

BUMPING HEADLINES

Bumping headlines occurs when the same point size is used for the headlines of two different stories. This confuses the reader and muddles the overall message. Varying the size of headlines enhances readability.

TRAPPED WHITE SPACE

Trapped white space occurs when a blank space appears on the page. It can occur between a headline and a graphic/illustration. In addition, white space can occur when a news story's text is too short to fill space down to the next headline.

Trapped white space is visually unattractive and detracts from the overall look of a page. Adjusting the size of graphics and illustrations or adding/deleting text so it fits within its allotted space can eliminate trapped white space

LEADING LINES

Within a photographic image, leading lines lead the eye to another point in the photo. Some examples of possible leading lines in photographs include a winding road, a path in the forest, or a fence that carries out to the horizon.

By attracting the viewer's eye to different points within the image, leading lines can help create a powerful composition that attracts the viewer's eye. Leading lines often work in conjunction with the rule of thirds, which divides the total image into nine distinct areas.

ILLUSTRATIONS

Illustrations can be photographs, graphics, or cartoons.

The typical issue of a student publication includes several photographs. The best photos complement and enhance the written copy. In many cases, a good photograph influences whether the reader chooses to read a particular story.

Graphics, when used properly, can explain a complicated subject visually. For example, a reader can understand a story with several statistics more easily if a bar graph or pie chart accompanies the story.

The editorial page usually employs the use of cartoons. By their nature, cartoons exaggerate and simplify subjects. They can create a strong response (both positive and negative) from readers.

CONSISTENCY AND CENTER OF VISUAL INTEREST

Consistency means helping the reader recognize, identify, and comprehend information within the publication.

The center of visual interest relates to the directional flow of reading. When designing a page, remember that most people view it in a "Z" pattern (starting in the upper-left corner, moving across to the right, then back to the left side of the page, going top to bottom).

EFFECTIVE ADVERTISING LAYOUT

Each display advertisement in a newspaper should be distinct, because several different ads often appear on the same page.

Copyright © Mometrix Media. You have been licensed one copy of this document for personal use only. Any other reproduction or redistribution is strictly prohibited. All rights reserved.
This content is provided for test preparation purposes only and does not imply an endorsement by Mometrix of any particular political, scientific, or religious point of view.

Artwork (photographs or graphics) should constitute the dominant element of a printed ad. Advertising first should seek to attract the reader's eye quickly, without using too much text. A good rule of thumb suggests that text should occupy no more than 20 percent of the space for each ad.

Emphasizing the local angle also can enhance the connection between advertisers and readers. As such, an ad for a sandwich shop close to campus might include a photo of the owner, or perhaps photos of students who work at the sandwich shop on weekends.

Display Advertising

In newspapers, display advertising includes text, photographs, and other graphic images. It appears on the same page as editorial content. In most cases, companies rather than individuals purchase display advertising.

With online publications, display advertising is generated by "banners" appearing above or next to editorial content on a Web page. The banners include still and animated images, and sometimes they include access to audio and video content.

Screen Printing

Screening is a printing method that squeezes ink through mesh fabric and a stencil. The angle and density of the screen determines how a graphic or photograph will reproduce on the printed page.

For four-color printing, the angle at which the screens intersect with the horizontal line of the press sheet differs for each color. The screen density (percentage of ink coverage allowed by a screen tint) also affects the overall look of the publication.

Copyright © Mometrix Media. You have been licensed one copy of this document for personal use only. Any other reproduction or redistribution is strictly prohibited. All rights reserved.
This content is provided for test preparation purposes only and does not imply an endorsement by Mometrix of any particular political, scientific, or religious point of view.

OSAT Practice Test

Want to take this practice test in an online interactive format?
Check out the online resources page, which includes interactive practice questions and much more: **mometrix.com/resources719/osatjourn137**

1. What was the legal significance of the 1735 trial of John Peter Zenger for the practice of journalism?

a. It established that local administrators were legally an extension of the British government and that their administration could not be legally criticized in print.
b. It established that an independent press, if not administered by a government authority, was inherently incapable of libel.
c. It established that advocating independence from Britain in print was an illegal act of rebellion.
d. It established that published material could not be considered libelous if it was based on fact.

2. Edward R. Murrow contributed to the development of American journalism in which of the following ways?

a. He established the first sensationalist tabloid television, focusing on lurid stories and "soft news" rather than headline news.
b. He publicly challenged the news establishment by pointing out that newsrooms would remain open to charges of bias as long they overwhelmingly employed only white men.
c. He actively reported on issues in the public interest and operated largely outside the traditional authority of a corporate newsroom.
d. He was the first television news anchor hired for his on-camera presence without having any significant background in reporting.

3. Which of the following best demonstrates the contribution made by Frederick Douglass to the development of the American press?

a. He established a children's press whose textbooks instilled generations of children with common republican values.
b. His founded a successful abolitionist newspaper that became widely read nationwide.
c. He wrote the first editorials by an African-American writer published in mainstream newspapers.
d. His libel trial established the first legal guidelines about publishing anti-slavery views in slaveholding states.

4. Which of the following is NOT a traditional role of the official press in an authoritarian society?

a. To act as an officially sanctioned "voice of the people" in states without democratic representation
b. To suppress news stories seen by the government as damaging to public order
c. To hire journalists from among favored associates of the ruling party
d. To champion government platforms

Copyright © Mometrix Media. You have been licensed one copy of this document for personal use only. Any other reproduction or redistribution is strictly prohibited. All rights reserved.
This content is provided for test preparation purposes only and does not imply an endorsement by Mometrix of any particular political, scientific, or religious point of view.

5. Which of the following is an example of how the medium affects the interpretation of the information reported?

a. The McCarthy hearings, which were followed closely by Americans in daily newspapers and television reports across the country
b. Statistics demonstrating that more Americans vote in nationally televised talent shows than vote for President
c. A report suggesting that a decline in book sales can be tied to the widespread availability of Internet access to American households.
d. The 1960 presidential debate in which radio listeners and television viewers came to two different conclusions about who had won

6. A student mentions during a class discussion that she has heard that the Spanish-American War marked a new role for the news media. How could a journalism teacher clarify the new role the media played in this war?

a. Have the students read a story by an American reporter and one by a Spanish reporter about the sinking of the USS Maine
b. Have the students read a factual account of the sinking of the USS Maine, and then show them an illustrated story that appeared in a Hearst newspaper
c. Compare an editorial from 1898 with a historical analysis of the war written after World War II
d. Explain the unprecedented authority President Roosevelt had to control unflattering editorials in daily newspapers

7. Which of the following best defines the significance of the Supreme Court case Hazelwood vs. Kuhlmeier?

a. It allows school authorities to censor student publications if they determine that the publications are not a "public forum" for student expression.
b. It states that a student newspaper serves a "valid pedagogical purpose" and as such enjoys absolute freedom of speech under the First Amendment.
c. It states that libel laws that apply to most newspapers do not apply to student newspapers, which are often written and edited by minors.
d. It affirms that underground and extracurricular publications are not official student publications, and as such, are not granted the legal First Amendment protections that an official student newspaper enjoys.

8. Which of the following is the strongest example of the press' function as a source of influence on public opinion?

a. The publication of a set of point-counterpoint columns about a series of local bond issues
b. The publication of the results of a public survey of confidence in government
c. An editorial advocating for the repeal of local zoning laws
d. A lead news story in which a government leader and a citizens' group leader are quoted offering opposite viewpoints on a proposed tax increase

Copyright © Mometrix Media. You have been licensed one copy of this document for personal use only. Any other reproduction or redistribution is strictly prohibited. All rights reserved.
This content is provided for test preparation purposes only and does not imply an endorsement by Mometrix of any particular political, scientific, or religious point of view.

9. Which of the following stories' messages is significantly distorted through the use of an irrelevant detail?

a. A soft profile about a local politician's part-time rock band that mentions his political differences with his band mates
b. A feature story of a local business owner running for political office in which she admits to having employed illegal laborers
c. A profile of several local Jewish and Arab business leaders that mentions ongoing hostilities in the Middle East
d. A news report about a local citizen protesting property tax rates that includes details about an immigration violation he committed twenty years previously

10. What is one important way that business interests influence the content of television news?

a. Private businesses purchase airtime for their commercials and can withdraw their financial support for news programs they find unacceptable.
b. Federal laws require broadcast networks to give equal airtime to political candidates of all the major political parties during an election, regardless of the political opinions of business leaders.
c. News programs often hire union production crews whose unions may have official opinions on public issues.
d. A company that has been unfavorably portrayed in a news program has a legal right to challenge on air the facts presented in the story.

11. What is one advantage that online journalism has over traditional print journalism?

a. Online journalism has a more established and rigorous standard of fairness than print journalism does.
b. Stories published through online media outlets can be published and corrected much more quickly than those published in print.
c. The ownership of online media outlets is usually more transparent than that of print journalism, enabling readers to identify any potential conflicts of interest.
d. Online media's revenue depends more heavily on advertising than print journalism does, which makes the online outlet more responsive to readers' input.

12. In class, a student argues that the improvement of television technology has made government more responsive to its citizens. Which example could a journalism teacher offer to help the student support her view?

a. Cable news networks now offer viewers 24-hour coverage of their government at work, rather than just highlights.
b. Visual effects technology now makes it more difficult to trust video footage produced by amateurs.
c. Only the most qualified broadcast journalists have access to the kind of expensive equipment that can produce a quality news program.
d. News networks are now forbidden to project an official presidential election winner before all national polls have closed in order to avoid influencing voters.

Copyright © Mometrix Media. You have been licensed one copy of this document for personal use only. Any other reproduction or redistribution is strictly prohibited. All rights reserved.
This content is provided for test preparation purposes only and does not imply an endorsement by Mometrix of any particular political, scientific, or religious point of view.

13. Which of the following would be the best video to show students in a lesson about the increased importance of the amateur in the production of television news?

a. Footage of a natural disaster aired on a cable news network that was shot and submitted by a viewer
b. Footage of a focus group in which viewers describe their preferences in news style
c. An interview done by a local broadcaster with an employee recently laid off by a local factory
d. A news story produced by a cable news station aired on both their channel and website

14. Students are discussing the intersection between money and television production. What point should a good journalism teacher reinforce about this subject?

a. Television programs with low budgets receive a much greater percentage of their revenue from advertising.
b. Public television receives its funding entirely from the federal government and so cannot be considered an objective source of information.
c. Because television is so expensive to produce, it is more responsive to viewer input than less-expensive forms of media.
d. All media, regardless of whether it is commercial or nonprofit, must depend on funding.

15. A journalism teacher asks students to locate the public financial information for each of the major television networks and daily newspapers. What is one lesson that students can learn from this exercise?

a. That media companies are primarily investment vehicles for their shareholders rather than sources of information
b. That media companies are for-profit enterprises and may have investments that create a conflict of interest in their news coverage
c. That media companies are typically structured as non-profit organizations, which subjects them to certain rules about what they can and cannot publish
d. That newspapers are taxed differently than television networks and are, therefore, not allowed to publish stories about subjects related to their companies' own business dealings

16. A class is asked to find and submit a news story for discussion. One student submits a news story from a website where all articles appear to be written by the same individual. What could a journalism instructor point out to the student to help him determine the reliability of the website as a source of information?

a. The website is required to register its financial and ownership information with a national database and should be investigated before it is used as a source.
b. The website does not have an editorial board and, therefore not subject to scrutiny over the objectivity or factuality of a story published there.
c. The website is clearly a subjective source of opinion rather than factual information.
d. The website is probably reliable because online journalists must demonstrate professional credibility before starting an individual website.

Copyright © Mometrix Media. You have been licensed one copy of this document for personal use only. Any other reproduction or redistribution is strictly prohibited. All rights reserved.
This content is provided for test preparation purposes only and does not imply an endorsement by Mometrix of any particular political, scientific, or religious point of view.

17. In a lesson on mass media, a teacher is showing commercials and analyzing their hidden messages. Which of the following is an example of a commercial that claims professional authority not supported by evidence?

a. A commercial selling pain relief featuring a professional basketball player who says he uses the product
b. A commercial for cold medicine narrated by a man in a doctor's coat
c. A commercial for a new toy showing footage of children playing happily with it
d. A commercial for a prepared food with testimonials by real consumers

18. Which of the following would be considered an ethical violation by a student photographer?

a. Superimposing a wide shot of a marching band practicing with a close-up of the drum major's face
b. Asking a student posing with his wrestling trophy to change his position in order to better frame the shot
c. Digitally removing the figure of a student from a candid group photo with the consent of all the students in the photo
d. Photographing the school principal in the school parking lot without her explicit permission

19. Which of the following would violate ethical principles in a student newspaper?

a. A photo of a fistfight in the parking lot after a football game
b. An article mentioning that a locally prominent advocate of abstinence-only sex education has a pregnant teenage daughter
c. A chart showing the total number of student arrests on drug charges in the last ten years broken down by year
d. An interview with the best friend of a student who has recently died

20. Which of the following accurately describes the 1969 Supreme Court decision Tinker v. Des Moines?

a. Students, when acting on their own behalf in public schools, have no constitutionally protected right to free speech.
b. Students have no protected right to publish material that advocates illegal activity or is sexually vulgar.
c. The First Amendment applies no differently in public schools than it does elsewhere in society.
d. School administrators who wish to regulate specific student speech must demonstrate a constitutionally valid reason for doing so.

21. Which of the following is an example of prior restraint?

a. A school newspaper advisor asks that a story not be published based on its possibly libelous content
b. A school administration prevents a school publication from going to press based on the controversial content of one of the articles
c. The subject of an unflattering article sues a publication on the grounds that it contains non-factual information
d. A school administration suspends a student journalist who has published an op-ed piece containing profanity

Copyright © Mometrix Media. You have been licensed one copy of this document for personal use only. Any other reproduction or redistribution is strictly prohibited. All rights reserved.
This content is provided for test preparation purposes only and does not imply an endorsement by Mometrix of any particular political, scientific, or religious point of view.

22. Which of the following is a legal responsibility not required of online journalists?

a. A responsibility to identify clearly when a company mentioned in an article has paid the writer of the article for the mention of the product
b. A responsibility to credit all stories originally published elsewhere
c. A responsibility to conform to state and federal libel laws
d. A responsibility to protect sources who wish to remain anonymous

23. A student newspaper editor plans to have a reporter interview the head football coach about rumors that the school's quarterback has been given leniency in an English class so that he can maintain the minimum grade point average required for participation in football games. Which of the following would be a useful suggestion for the editor under the circumstances?

a. That the assigned reporter should be a student with no relationship to any of the involved parties: the teacher, the coach, or the quarterback
b. That an accompanying editorial should run in the same issue of the newspaper pointing out that a student should always be given the benefit of the doubt in matters of ethics
c. That the reporter should interview as many sources as possible, including those with different opinions about the rumors
d. That the story should be cancelled based on the probability that any given student journalist will have a relationship with one of the two parties, preventing objectivity.

24. A student journalist wishes to write an article on a student who has recently been hospitalized for an overdose of illegal drugs. Which of the following would be unethical to include in the article?

a. Opinions from students who believe that drugs should be legalized
b. Quotations from students present at the party where the incident took place
c. Statistics based on a survey of current students about the rates of drug consumption on campus
d. An interview with the student's doctor about the student's welfare

25. Which of the following would be the best resource for a student journalist interested in researching high school graduation rates by state?

a. The website of the Texas Educational Authority
b. A chart from the United Nations educational organization
c. An interview with the school district superintendent
d. A database from the Department of Education

26. A student reporter is doing a report on brands of athletic equipment used in her school's athletics program. She reports to a journalism advisor that she has discovered an article online about sports equipment and would like to cite the article in her report. Which of the following would prevent the article from being an appropriate resource for her report?

a. The website the article appears on is run by a sports-equipment company.
b. The article's author is a former professional athlete.
c. The article focuses only on the brand of equipment used primarily at the reporter's school rather than several brands.
d. The article cites personal testimonies from users of athletic equipment rather than scientific studies about the equipment's efficacy.

Copyright © Mometrix Media. You have been licensed one copy of this document for personal use only. Any other reproduction or redistribution is strictly prohibited. All rights reserved.
This content is provided for test preparation purposes only and does not imply an endorsement by Mometrix of any particular political, scientific, or religious point of view.

27. A letter to a school newspaper complains that the last several sports sections have focused on tennis, a sport whose school team consists almost entirely of white students. What would be an appropriate response by the newspaper staff?

a. To publish the letter in the next issue, along with a rebuttal from the reporter responsible for tennis coverage, pointing out that the tennis team is having a winning season
b. To set a new requirement to have at least one photograph of a minority student in each sports section
c. To assess the paper's coverage of extracurricular activities and set a new policy of covering at least three sports in every issue
d. To publish a written apology from the staff and to not publish tennis coverage in the next two issues of the paper

28. A student reporter is scheduled to attend a press conference at which the state's US Senator will be speaking. Which of the following is the best advice for an advisor to give the reporter?

a. Take a tape recorder instead of a notebook since the Senator's answers to his questions may be quite long.
b. Practice active listening skills and confident body language to make the Senator more comfortable.
c. Ask multi-part questions in order to solicit the most thoughtful responses.
d. Plan several questions to ask the Senator and prioritize them.

29. Which of the following could be used in an article without direct attribution to a person?

a. A quotation about student dropouts by a well-known public figure
b. Criticism of school dropouts by the school principal
c. Government statistics on high school dropout rates by state
d. A quotation from a famous poem about the lives of uneducated young people

30. A student reporter has interviewed several people for a feature article he is writing about exchange students at school. The rough draft of the article is twice as long as the space allotted for it, and the reporter is struggling to cut it to an appropriate length. What is the best way for him to assess what should be cut to keep the article within the required length?

a. He should ensure that he has several points of view represented but no redundant ones.
b. He should ensure that his article has more quotations from people who share his point of view than from people who disagree with him.
c. He should ensure that only students are represented in the article since they are the primary audience for it.
d. He should sort the sources and cut half of them at random in order to ensure his article does not betray inadvertent bias.

Copyright © Mometrix Media. You have been licensed one copy of this document for personal use only. Any other reproduction or redistribution is strictly prohibited. All rights reserved.
This content is provided for test preparation purposes only and does not imply an endorsement by Mometrix of any particular political, scientific, or religious point of view.

31. Which of the following could be used as a classroom exercise to introduce ideas about gathering information for news articles in an unbiased way?

a. A free writing assignment in which students must assume the personas of various people who might be useful in creating an article
b. A brainstorming exercise in which students create lists of potential interviewees and list a different reason for each interviewee's value to the story
c. An exercise in which students create two different outlines for the same article, detailing the flow of information presented
d. An exercise in which students divide into pairs and interview one another about the same subject

32. An editorial is characterized primarily by its being:

a. An unbiased account of facts
b. The point of view of one identified writer
c. The official opinion of the entire newspaper staff
d. Factually based but not as timely as a news story

33. Which of the following would be the LEAST appropriate story for a student publication?

a. A feature story on college scholarships for student athletes
b. A news story on the school football team's winning season
c. An investigation into discrepancies in funding for various local school football programs
d. A report on the progress of the new local professional football team

34. A student is writing a feature article on students involved in unusual extracurricular activities. Which of the following would be the LEAST appropriate item to include in this article?

a. A photo of a student who is learning to fly single-engine planes
b. A quotation from a student who feels that school prevents him from devoting himself more fully to his pursuit of an Olympic dream
c. A quotation from a teacher who feels that the school is funding extracurricular activities at the expense of academics
d. A complaint from a teacher who feels that students who participate in extracurricular activities do poorly in class

35. A student journalist plans to write a story about exchange students enrolled in local high schools. Who among the following sources does NOT need attribution in this story?

a. A spokesperson for a local exchange student organization that provided statistics for the article
b. An exchange student who is quoted on her experiences
c. A student who resents the presence of exchange students but wishes to remain anonymous
d. The school principal, who is a public figure in the local community

Copyright © Mometrix Media. You have been licensed one copy of this document for personal use only. Any other reproduction or redistribution is strictly prohibited. All rights reserved.
This content is provided for test preparation purposes only and does not imply an endorsement by Mometrix of any particular political, scientific, or religious point of view.

36. A student journalist is writing a caption for a photo depicting a basketball player for the school's team dunking a basket. The article is a news story about the previous Friday night's game. Which of the following would be the best caption for this photo?

a. "Steven Jones dunks the ball in Friday's game. He is planning to attend the University of Texas on a basketball scholarship next year."
b. "Steven Jones dunks the ball after a harrowing first quarter against Central High. McKinley went on to win 63-48."
c. "Steven Jones dunks the ball."
d. "After a harrowing first quarter against Central High, McKinley went on to win 63-48."

37. Which of the following exercises would be useful in teaching beginning journalism students about the differences among types of journalistic writing (e.g. newspaper, television, online)?

a. Have students write an article for print, and then shoot videos of them reading it for broadcast
b. Provide a list of published or broadcast sentences from news stories and have students assign them to a category
c. Have students find articles online and copyedit them for broadcast and traditional print formats
d. Have students transcribe a story broadcast on local news and check it for errors in proper inverted pyramid style

38. A student journalist is having trouble sorting through her notes for a news article. She has used the inverted pyramid format but finds that a particularly useful quotation is lost when she cuts the story for length. How could a journalism teacher best advise her to proceed?

a. Ask her to reorganize the story in chronological order, and then cut anything that falls beyond the length limit.
b. Accept that she must lose the quotation since it falls below the cutoff point for the length of her story
c. Include the quotation in an earlier paragraph that quotes a different interviewee
d. Edit the lead of the story so that the desired quotation is more directly relevant to the main thrust of the story and then reorganize the story in inverted-pyramid style

39. Which point should a journalism advisor stress when helping student journalists to write appropriate two-line headlines?

a. Avoid awkward line breaks
b. Never use direct quotations
c. Avoid using more than one subject and verb
d. Keep all subjects on the same line

40. In class, a journalism student asks an advisor what the importance is of maintaining a stylebook for a newspaper staff. Which example could the advisor cite in illustrating for the student the situations in which a stylebook is useful for journalists?

a. A student does not know which interviewed source to use when cutting a story for length
b. A student is not sure whether using a quotation from a subject violates federal obscenity rules
c. A student does not how to refer to a teacher with a PhD when quoting her in a story
d. A student is not sure what the best placement for an ad is within an issue of the newspaper

Copyright © Mometrix Media. You have been licensed one copy of this document for personal use only. Any other reproduction or redistribution is strictly prohibited. All rights reserved.
This content is provided for test preparation purposes only and does not imply an endorsement by Mometrix of any particular political, scientific, or religious point of view.

41. A student is writing the first draft of an article. The article is too long to fit in the space allotted for it, but the student observes that the sentence count is not very high. What advice could be given to help her improve her draft?

a. Use shorter words to avoid overwhelming the audience.
b. Remove entire paragraphs rather than sentences in order to maintain cohesion within the article..
c. Combine paragraphs to encourage the development of ideas within the story.
d. Use active voice verbs and avoid unnecessary words that do not add information to the story.

42. A student reporter has interviewed a high school senior who provides computer-programming services to the school district. The reporter is himself an amateur programmer and is in the planning stages of his article. What advice should he be given before writing it?

a. To avoid any jargon that might be unfamiliar to an uninformed reader
b. To warn the audience in the first paragraph that the article may contain difficult words
c. To keep the article as short as possible since it mentions technical subjects
d. To write in the passive voice to avoid overwhelming the audience

43. What is one reason to introduce students to historical articles by renowned journalists?

a. To provide a better understanding of how modern journalism operates according to an entirely different set of ethical standards than early 20th-century journalism
b. To develop an appreciation in students of the development of journalistic standards through the decades
c. To develop an appreciation in students of how online culture has influenced journalistic writing practices of the last 10 years
d. To help students distinguish between the personal essays of early journalism and the fact-based articles of today

44. Which of the following developments of recent decades has had a controversial effect on copyright issues?

a. The increased use of color photography rather than black-and-white
b. The development of centralized wire services such as the Associated Press
c. The use of word processors rather than dictation to write articles
d. The introduction of digital files as a way to save photographic work

45. Consistent legal standards for privacy expectations apply to all individuals:

a. Without any exceptions
b. With the exception of foreign nationals
c. With the exception of public figures and celebrities
d. As long as they are adults over the age of 18

46. Which of the following lenses would be most appropriate for a sports journalist covering a soccer game?

a. Macro
b. Fisheye
c. Telephoto
d. Sift control

Copyright © Mometrix Media. You have been licensed one copy of this document for personal use only. Any other reproduction or redistribution is strictly prohibited. All rights reserved.
This content is provided for test preparation purposes only and does not imply an endorsement by Mometrix of any particular political, scientific, or religious point of view.

47. A good photo caption should:

a. Tie the information in the photo to the information in the accompanying article
b. Describe the action taking place in the photo
c. List the individuals in the photo
d. Reproduce the main thrust of the article's lead paragraph

48. How should a student newspaper staff ensure that its photographic coverage represents the entire student body fairly and accurately?

a. Create a checklist of minority groups and publish one representative from each group in each issue of the paper.
b. Create a policy of including as many students as possible in the staff's photographic coverage.
c. Avoid publishing any individual photographs of students in case they are interpreted as unflattering.
d. Make sure that the newspaper staff itself is diverse to ensure that each of its own ethnic groups is represented in photographic coverage.

49. What is the "rule of thirds" as it applies to photography?

a. The f-stop must be increased by one-third for each 10 meters between the camera and subject.
b. The amount of actual light on a subject will register as only one-third as bright on film.
c. For every increase in shutter speed, the f-stop on a camera should be decreased by one-third.
d. Important compositional elements should align with the intersecting points one-third of the distance from any edge in a photograph.

50. When would it be appropriate to employ a shallow depth of field when taking a photograph?

a. When photographing a subject very far away
b. When photographing a subject in motion
c. When the photographer wishes to isolate an important element from the background in a photograph
d. When photographing several objects at different distances from the camera lens

51. A student wishes to scan a photograph for possible use in a story but does not yet know how the photograph will be used. What advice should he be given to ensure that the scanned photograph suits as many purposes as possible?

a. Scan the photograph at a high resolution so that it can be used at many sizes without degradation of quality.
b. Crop the photograph when scanning so that the file size is not too big for the photograph to be stored digitally.
c. Desaturate the image when scanning to preserve the image's contrast.
d. Shrink the photograph to the size most likely to be used in print when saving the file.

Copyright © Mometrix Media. You have been licensed one copy of this document for personal use only. Any other reproduction or redistribution is strictly prohibited. All rights reserved.
This content is provided for test preparation purposes only and does not imply an endorsement by Mometrix of any particular political, scientific, or religious point of view.

52. What is a leading line in a photographic image?

a. The imaginary lines that divide a photograph into nine equal rectangles for compositional purposes
b. The line of code in the digital file that contains information about the color and resolution of the image
c. A strong compositional line in a photograph that directs the eye to the main subject
d. The imaginary lines marking off the outer 10% of a photograph that will not be visible in a printed newspaper

53. Which of the following would be the LEAST appropriate image to include in a photo essay about a high school marching band?

a. A posed headshot of the band leader
b. A close up of a group of instruments in a corner before band practice
c. An action shot of a trombonist playing during halftime
d. A candid shot of three musicians resting between songs

54. Due to budget constraints, a high school newspaper is now limited to publishing only 12 pages per issue. Which of the following design measures should be taken to make the publication look as professional as possible under the circumstances?

a. Divide the newspaper into three distinct sections, each with a unique look and layout, to mimic the look of a larger paper
b. Limit the number of typefaces and colors used to maintain a consistent style throughout the publication
c. Place the first few paragraphs of as many stories as possible on the first page with jumps to continuing coverage on the last pages
d. Decrease the size of headlines and photos in order to increase the amount of space devoted to article text

55. Which of the following publication types would be best suited to a layout consisting of a two-page spread with a central large photograph, several smaller photographs surrounding the central one, and text boxes on the outside edges of each page?

a. Student art publication
b. Literary magazine
c. Yearbook
d. Broadsheet newspaper

Copyright © Mometrix Media. You have been licensed one copy of this document for personal use only. Any other reproduction or redistribution is strictly prohibited. All rights reserved.
This content is provided for test preparation purposes only and does not imply an endorsement by Mometrix of any particular political, scientific, or religious point of view.

56. The following is a mockup of the front page of the next planned issue of a school newspaper. Which of the following would be the most effective change to make in terms of design?

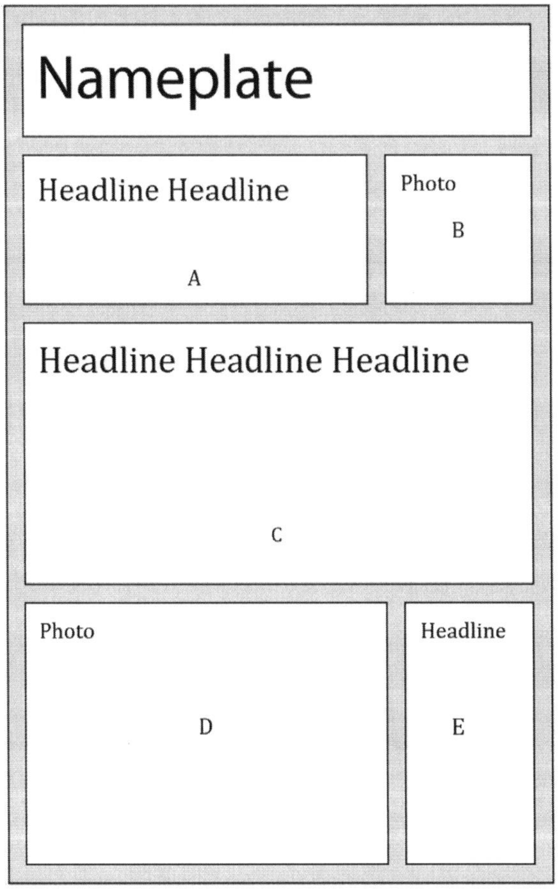

a. Switch the placement of article E and photo B.
b. Move article C up on the page and move article A and photo B down on the page.
c. Eliminate photo B and spread article A over three columns.
d. Move article E to another page and replace it with a photo.

57. A student reporter has conducted a survey of high school seniors about the number of hours a week most commonly worked among those with part-time jobs. Which of the following would best represent this data in a graphic to accompany the article?

a. A pie chart
b. A bar graph
c. A pictograph
d. A line graph

Copyright © Mometrix Media. You have been licensed one copy of this document for personal use only. Any other reproduction or redistribution is strictly prohibited. All rights reserved.
This content is provided for test preparation purposes only and does not imply an endorsement by Mometrix of any particular political, scientific, or religious point of view.

58. The following is a mockup of a two-page spread in a yearbook. Which of the following areas is problematic?

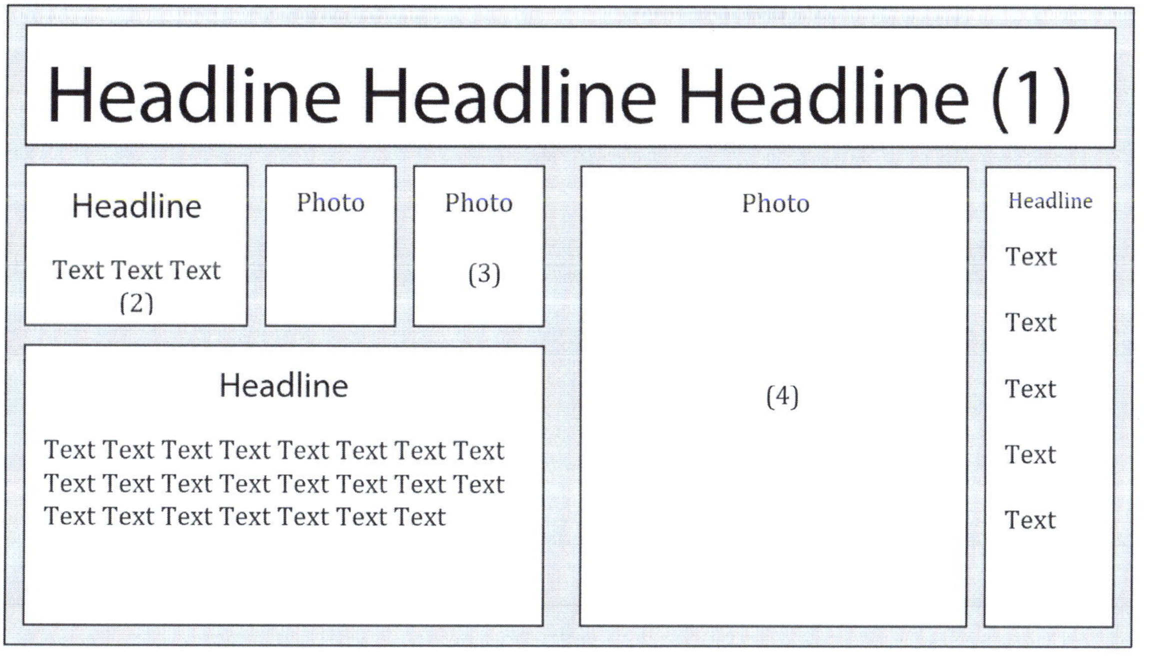

a. 1
b. 2
c. 3
d. 4

59. Which of the following functions would be the best use of desktop publishing software in publishing a student newspaper?

a. Designing graphics and artwork
b. Writing the text of the articles
c. Adjusting the color and cropping photos
d. Arranging the stories, photos, and masthead on the page

60. Photographs taken by photojournalists like Dorothea Lange during the Great Depression were historically significant because they:

a. Inspired President Roosevelt's New Deal programs
b. Were the first examples of nationally-published documentary photography
c. Published the reality of economic desperation around the nation
d. Were the first published works by women photojournalists

61. A student has produced a mockup of a sports section page consisting of four articles and an advertisement but finds that the articles do not fill the page entirely. Which of the following would be the best suggestion to offer him to improve the look of his page?

a. Support one of the stories with a photo.
b. Increase the size of the advertisement.
c. Add length to each of the articles.
d. Increase the size of the smallest headline.

Copyright © Mometrix Media. You have been licensed one copy of this document for personal use only. Any other reproduction or redistribution is strictly prohibited. All rights reserved.
This content is provided for test preparation purposes only and does not imply an endorsement by Mometrix of any particular political, scientific, or religious point of view.

62. A student has taken a color photograph that is appropriately proportioned for a planned article. The photograph will be reproduced, however, in black and white. Which of the following kinds of image manipulation would be appropriate under the circumstances?

a. Solarization
b. Cropping
c. File format conversion
d. Saturation and contrast

63. Which of the following is an important universal rule for students to learn about the front page of a newspaper issue?

a. Maximize the number of photos on the front page.
b. Never run an advertisement on the front page.
c. Front pages are typically characterized by at least 10 stories.
d. Op-ed pieces should be featured at the bottom of a front page.

64. A student is designing an ad for a local coffee shop that is trying to increase its business with students. The ad most likely to be effective with students would include:

a. A photograph of the owner
b. A freehand drawing of a cup of coffee
c. A color photograph of a student at the coffee shop
d. A logo derived from the logo of a soft drink brand popular with students

65. A script font would be most appropriate in which of the following situations?

a. In the nameplate for a student newspaper
b. In a bar graph within a newspaper article
c. Within the body text in a yearbook spread
d. As the headline of a yearbook spread

66. The staff of a school newspaper plans to publish the content of each issue on a website. The staff editor wants to scan each page of the issue and post it as a separate page on the website. Which of the following is NOT a disadvantage of this strategy?

a. Articles that continue on another page make navigating the site awkward.
b. The process of uploading the data onto the server will be far more time-consuming than simply uploading each article and photo.
c. Saving the articles as graphics files rather than text consumes more space on the web server.
d. Saving the articles in this way will make it impossible for readers to scan them electronically for keywords.

67. The development of cable television in the 1970s led to which of the following programming changes?

a. Television programming became privatized in the United States.
b. There was an increase in the number and specificity of television channels.
c. Television programming was deregulated.
d. Programming began to be broadcast 24 hours a day.

Copyright © Mometrix Media. You have been licensed one copy of this document for personal use only. Any other reproduction or redistribution is strictly prohibited. All rights reserved.
This content is provided for test preparation purposes only and does not imply an endorsement by Mometrix of any particular political, scientific, or religious point of view.

68. President Franklin D. Roosevelt's "Fireside Chats" were known for:

a. Making use of radio to reach a national audience.
b. Passing encoded messages to counterespionage operatives.
c. Being the first time a US president appeared on television.
d. Being the first successful use of mass media in a national election campaign.

69. One way that writing for print differs from broadcast writing is that a writer for print:

a. Has less flexibility to use alliteration and poetic language
b. Must take more care to avoid repetitive words
c. Can present more information in a denser writing style without confusing the audience
d. Always uses the present tense, whereas a broadcast writer uses the past tense

70. One principle that is important to remember in writing a script for news broadcast is that:

a. Viewers tend to pay more attention to news broadcasters with whom they can identify.
b. The audio narrative must be capable of standing alone without the accompanying visual information.
c. The primary function of a broadcast is to confirm community standards, not to challenge them.
d. Viewers have only one chance to register the information presented to them.

71. Which of the following accurately describes the role of a large market news broadcast director?

a. Handles the details of camera placement and staff activities
b. Controls the on-air video switcher and technical equipment
c. Reads recorded stories on-air and conducts interviews
d. Compiles news stories from recorded videotape, adding music and graphics

72. A journalism teacher has assigned his students a project to shoot a video interview with a parent and edit b-roll into the final video. Which of the following is an example of b-roll?

a. A fade to black between shots of the student's mother telling a story
b. A silent shot of a shelf of bowling trophies won by a student's father
c. A shot of the interview that includes both the student and his father
d. A shot of the student alone asking her mother questions

73. What is one restriction on the production of broadcast news that does not apply to the production of print media?

a. There are a specific number of stories that can be presented in any given broadcast.
b. Because broadcast news is shown nightly but stories take time to produce, all stories must be produced far in advance of their airing.
c. Broadcast news is legally required to devote a particular percentage of its programming time to advertising, but print media is subject to no such requirements.
d. Regulations restrict the content that can be legally presented in a broadcast production.

Copyright © Mometrix Media. You have been licensed one copy of this document for personal use only. Any other reproduction or redistribution is strictly prohibited. All rights reserved.
This content is provided for test preparation purposes only and does not imply an endorsement by Mometrix of any particular political, scientific, or religious point of view.

74. A journalism teacher has assigned his students to produce a short video featuring a friend. They are to interview the student on camera, shoot relevant locations, and employ a visual transition technique in the video. Which of the following places would be the best place to use a transition?

a. During the student's questions
b. During the friend's answers
c. Between a wide shot of the friend and a close up of the friend
d. Between a shot of the friend and a shot of the friend's home

75. A journalism teacher is conducting a unit on broadcast news with her students. She asks them to watch a broadcast of a local news program and list the order and running time of each story. What purpose could by served by this exercise?

a. Students can evaluate how stories are prioritized.
b. Students can analyze how advertising affects the content of the broadcast.
c. Students can assess how the anchors' tone changes according to which story they are presenting.
d. Students can analyze how time constraints on a broadcast force broadcasters to eliminate less-important stories.

76. What is the purpose of offering a contract rate to advertisers who agree to place ads in a school newspaper throughout the year?

a. It will decrease the cost in acquisition time and energy per ad for the staff.
b. The contract will allow the newspaper ultimately to run less advertising.
c. It will give the paper an appearance of corporate sponsorship, which will increase its credibility with readers.
d. It will enable the staff to track the effectiveness of advertising throughout the year.

77. A newspaper staff is planning to solicit advertisements from local businesses. Which of the following would be most helpful for staffers to present to business owners when making their case?

a. An advertisement the business has placed elsewhere, showing that the staffers are familiar with the business
b. Statistics showing that businesses that place adds in the paper increase their business with students by 15%
c. A recent copy of the paper, illustrating its quality
d. A receipt from the printer, showing the number of copies produced of the most recent issue of the paper

78. Which of the following would be the LEAST effective way of improving the look of an advertisement?

a. Adding a graphic to catch the reader's interest
b. Adding contact information for the business
c. Making the type smaller to draw the reader in
d. Printing it in color rather than black-and-white

Copyright © Mometrix Media. You have been licensed one copy of this document for personal use only. Any other reproduction or redistribution is strictly prohibited. All rights reserved.
This content is provided for test preparation purposes only and does not imply an endorsement by Mometrix of any particular political, scientific, or religious point of view.

79. Which of the following sales techniques would be considered unethical for a newspaper staffer to use when soliciting businesses for advertisements in a student newspaper?

a. Suggesting that the business is popular with students
b. Telling the business owner that the staffer himself frequents her establishment
c. Offering a discount if the owner purchases an ad in every issue of the newspaper
d. Guaranteeing a 5% increase in business from students

80. How can a yearbook staff incorporate advertising into a yearbook to best ensure that students view the ads?

a. Incorporate ads into editorials endorsing the products
b. Group all advertisements into their own section, with an entry in the yearbook's table of contents
c. Place the ads on pages that feature candid photographs of students
d. Group all advertisements together in a stand-alone supplement to the yearbook

81. A classified ad is a suitable choice for a business:

a. When the business has artwork it wishes to incorporate in the ad
b. When the business's advertising budget is large
c. When it wishes to attract the attention of a new audience
d. When the potential audience for the ad is already seeking a particular product.

82. The staff of a high school newspaper decides to set up a free distribution box for the paper on the main street of the local town. What is the main purpose that would be served by doing this?

a. It would reinforce connections between students and the local community.
b. It would broaden the audience for the advertisers.
c. It would allow public input on the content on the school paper.
d. It would expose the writing of student journalists to a professional audience.

83. The primary role of a school newspaper advisor is:

a. To exercise prior restraint over student writing
b. To select and assign articles to student journalists
c. To educate students about the practice of journalism and consult on production problems
d. To copyedit articles and oversee photographic work

84. This year, the editor of a high school yearbook has decided to have staffers keep a group notebook that includes mockup layouts throughout various stages of editing. What purpose does this notebook serve?

a. It enables credit to be given to the correct staffer for successful ideas.
b. It encourages competition among staffers in order to prepare them for professional journalistic life.
c. It enables the staff to note which ideas are unsuccessful in case they return to the same project in the future.
d. It gives future yearbook staff a goal to which to aspire.

Copyright © Mometrix Media. You have been licensed one copy of this document for personal use only. Any other reproduction or redistribution is strictly prohibited. All rights reserved.
This content is provided for test preparation purposes only and does not imply an endorsement by Mometrix of any particular political, scientific, or religious point of view.

85. Part of the grade in a journalism class is determined by peer reviews. How does having students help determine other students' grades help students to become better journalists?

a. Students learn that journalism is a collaborative effort rather than an individual one.
b. Students learn that the quality of one's work will always be evaluated partly by others' preconceived notions about one's personality.
c. Students learn that the ultimate goal of journalism is to try to please as many groups as possible in the community.
d. Students learn that the opinions of readers are ultimately less important than those of fellow journalists.

86. What is chief benefit of a class exercise in which small groups of students work together to determine an outline of an editorial?

a. Students learn the value of healthy competition.
b. Students learn to work collaboratively.
c. Students learn to appreciate the freedom to work alone without obstruction.
d. Students learn to choose writing partners who share their points of view as much as possible.

87. When would it be most productive for a journalism advisor to employ a contest situation on a newspaper staff?

a. To reward students for quality photographic work
b. To encourage students to come up with as many potential article topics as possible
c. To reward students for improving the quality of their first drafts
d. To encourage students to find and correct typographical errors before the newspaper is sent to press

88. At the beginning of the school year, veteran staffers of a high school newspaper are meeting to determine which new applicants to take on staff. The paper's staff, as it is currently composed, lacks ethnic diversity. How could the newspaper's advisor best help to guide the selection process?

a. Establish a list of minority ethnic groups and socioeconomic backgrounds, and make sure one representative from each group is chosen for the staff.
b. Ask the staffers to compile a list of weaknesses in their previous news coverage and identify potential new staffers who could strengthen it.
c. Advise the staffers to compile a short-list of quality candidates, and select them at random to eliminate any inadvertent bias.
d. Assume a main role in the selection process since staffers are likely to be unaware of their biases.

89. In the monthly editorial meeting, the staff decides that the next issue's editorial will be about the grade-point system currently used in the school. Two students disagree strongly over the issue. How could an advisor help resolve the stalemate as it affects the editorial?

a. Ask the staff to come up with an alternative editorial on which all staffers agree and propose having the two disagreeing students write a point-counterpoint piece.
b. Assign the writing of the editorial to the managing editor whose opinion on the issue is clear.
c. Ask the lowest-ranking staffer to recuse herself from the editorial process.
d. Advise the staff to format the editorial so that it represents both points of view.

Copyright © Mometrix Media. You have been licensed one copy of this document for personal use only. Any other reproduction or redistribution is strictly prohibited. All rights reserved.
This content is provided for test preparation purposes only and does not imply an endorsement by Mometrix of any particular political, scientific, or religious point of view.

90. Two student reporters approach a newspaper advisor with a complaint that the student editor of the newspaper is exerting inordinate control over the selection and content of articles to be published. What would be the best action for the advisor to take under the circumstances?

a. Eliminate the editor position and replace it with a majority-vote process involving the entire newspaper staff.
b. Set up a meeting with all three students at which the advisor acts as a facilitator.
c. Remind the reporters of the editor's absolute right to maintain a coherent vision for the newspaper.
d. Redelegate the editor's responsibilities to another student.

91. A school administrator has learned that an op-ed critical of the school's suspension policy is planned for the next issue of the school paper. The administrator is angry. What course of action should the newspaper advisor recommend to the paper's editor?

a. A meeting between the newspaper staff and the principal to explain the staff's position and listen to her concerns
b. An appointment with a lawyer to obtain a legal letter outlining the staff's right to publish
c. An e-mail to the principal stating unequivocally that the staff will be publishing the op-ed piece as planned
d. An abandonment of the op-ed for something more acceptable to the administration

92. Why should a high school journalism advisor work to solicit partnerships with working journalists in the community?

a. It may help students to find jobs after high school.
b. It will help students gain access to events requiring press credentials.
c. It will enable students to seek advice and mentorship from more experienced journalists.
d. Having outside partnerships will give the school newspaper ethical leverage when dealing with administration officials.

Refer to the following for questions 93–95:

A student at a local high school has recently committed suicide. The school newspaper's staff is meeting to determine how to handle the news.

93. Which of the following legal principles is most likely to cause challenges in determining how to cover the information?

a. Use of anonymous sources
b. Libel
c. Invasion of privacy
d. Prior review

94. The student assigned to write the article knew the deceased student, having been in several classes with him. What advice will a good journalism advisor offer him in this particular case?

a. To avoid interviewing those closest to the story
b. To support all his interviews with statistics
c. To interview as many sources as possible
d. To avoid bias in his writing

Copyright © Mometrix Media. You have been licensed one copy of this document for personal use only. Any other reproduction or redistribution is strictly prohibited. All rights reserved.
This content is provided for test preparation purposes only and does not imply an endorsement by Mometrix of any particular political, scientific, or religious point of view.

95. Ultimately, the staff decides to name the student in the article but not list the cause of death. Having created a solution to their immediate ethical problem, what is the next best step for them to take?

a. Include an editorial addressing the problem of student suicide in the next issue of the newspaper.
b. Invite representatives of the deceased student to speak to the newspaper staff, offering their opinion on the staff's action.
c. Compile a graph of student-death statistics listing cause of death for young people nationwide.
d. Create a stylebook that lists clearly the staff's policy on addressing student deaths.

Refer to the following for questions 96–98:

> A school newspaper is preparing a feature article on the boys' soccer captain who has just received a soccer scholarship to college. A student photographer is assigned to photograph him on the soccer field after school to create photos to accompany the article.

96. Which of the following would necessarily constitute unethical behavior on the part of the photographer?

a. Asking the captain to replay a shot on goal he took in a previous game at which the photographer was not present
b. Cropping the photograph after printing it, to achieve better composition
c. Adjusting the color of the printed photo to increase the contrast
d. Arranging for the captain to pose with a soccer ball

97. The photojournalist takes a series of photos of the captain on the soccer field. One photo taken shows poor color when it is printed: the entire background is white, and much of the detail of the captain's uniform is missing. What should the photographer have changed when taking the photograph?

a. Increased the f-stop
b. Decreased the aperture size
c. Used a telephoto lens
d. Used a flash

98. Which of the following would be the best caption for a photo of the captain shooting a goal?

a. "Marcus Johnson takes a shot on goal."
b. "Marcus Johnson, GHS student"
c. "Marcus Johnson won a scholarship to Iowa State University. In his spare time, Marcus also likes playing football."
d. "Marcus Johnson takes a practice shot on goal. Johnson recently won a scholarship to Iowa State University."

Copyright © Mometrix Media. You have been licensed one copy of this document for personal use only. Any other reproduction or redistribution is strictly prohibited. All rights reserved.
This content is provided for test preparation purposes only and does not imply an endorsement by Mometrix of any particular political, scientific, or religious point of view.

Refer to the following for questions 99–100:

The following is a proposed layout for a 2-page layout in a high school yearbook:

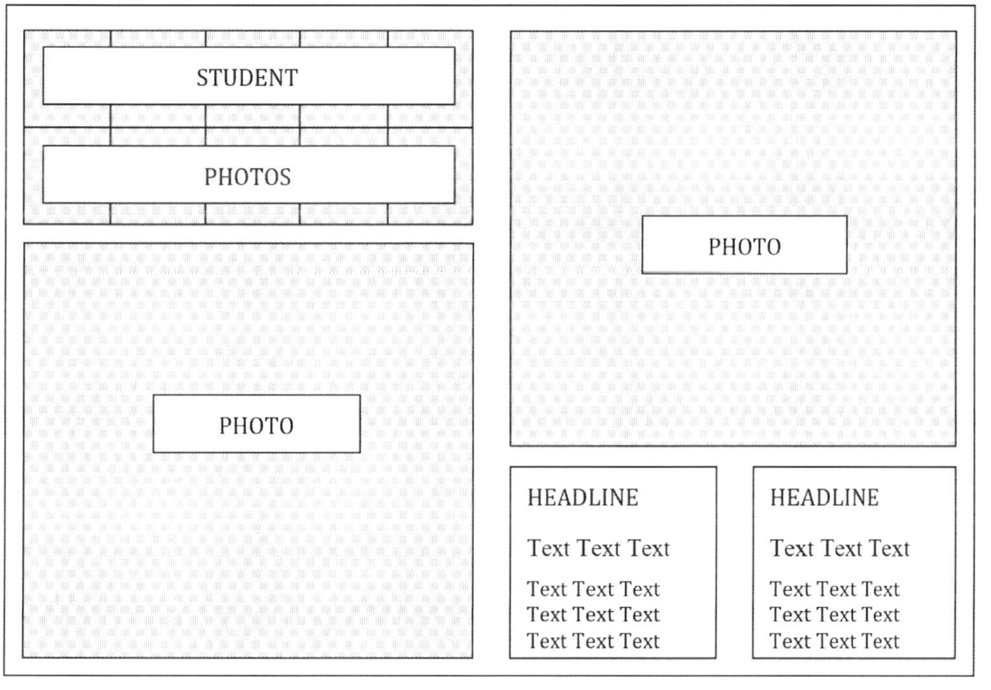

99. Which of the following changes would be most effective in increasing the visual interest of the page?

a. Switching the section of student photos with the large photo on the left page
b. Switching the two articles with the large photo above them
c. Switching the left-hand article with the left half of the group of student photos
d. Making each of the articles two columns long rather than one

100. Which computer program would be best to use to change the layout of this yearbook?

a. A word processor
b. Desktop publishing software
c. Photo-manipulation software
d. A database program

Copyright © Mometrix Media. You have been licensed one copy of this document for personal use only. Any other reproduction or redistribution is strictly prohibited. All rights reserved.
This content is provided for test preparation purposes only and does not imply an endorsement by Mometrix of any particular political, scientific, or religious point of view.

Answer Key and Explanations

1. D: Zenger's trial represented a departure from the traditional English practice of awarding a guilty verdict in libel trials by proving simply that the defendant published the words in question, not that the words were untrue. Option A suggests that Zenger was acting illegally by publishing criticism of Governor Cosby, the alleged libel for which Zenger was sued. In fact, a 'not guilty' verdict was returned. Option B, that an independent press was determined to be incapable of libel, is incorrect since the concept of libel is still very much with us. Option C, that it was illegal to advocate colonial independence in print, is irrelevant to the Zenger case; Zenger was accused of libeling Governor Cosby, not of advocating independence. Option D describes the significance of the case correctly; criticizing a public official in print did not itself constitute libel. Option D is the best answer to this question.

2. C: Murrow was known for his career as an independent advocate of the public interest and his practice of actively investigating and reporting the news rather than simply announcing it. Option A, that Murrow established the first tabloid brand of television, is not true; Murrow was known for his in-depth reporting on public issues. Option B, that he publicly advocated more newsroom diversity, is not something that one would associate with Murrow. Option C, that he reported on public issues and worked outside the traditional structure of a corporate newsroom, is true; Murrow was known as a serious journalist rather than simply a mouthpiece. Option D, that Murrow was hired for his presence rather than his experience, is inaccurate. In fact, Murrow was well known for the seriousness with which he approached the role of a broadcast journalist. Option C is the best answer choice.

3. B: Frederick Douglass, while known for his autobiography, also played a significant role in the anti-slavery movement through his work in journalism. Option A, that he established a children's press, is inaccurate; he often referred to his own experiences reading The Columbian Orator, a widely read schoolbook, but did not establish a children's press of his own. Option B, that he established a successful abolitionist newspaper, is consistent with what we know about Douglass; he did establish an abolitionist newspaper, the North Star, in 1847. Option C, that he wrote the first editorials by an African-American writer published in a mainstream newspaper, is not accurate. His contribution to journalism was primarily as a publisher and editor. Option D, that his libel trial produced the first guidelines about publishing antislavery views in slaveholding states, is inaccurate. William Lloyd Garrison, another abolitionist publisher, was accused of libel, not Douglass. Option B is the best answer choice.

4. A: The role of the official press under authoritarian regimes, unlike in democratic societies, is not to inform the public and publish in its interest but to support the ruling party and to suppress dissenting views. Option A, to act as a "voice of the people," describes the role of the press as that of a government watchdog, a role we know to associate with media in democratic societies, not authoritarian ones. Option B, to suppress news stories seen as damaging to public order, is an action we do associate with the "official" press of an oppressive regime. Option C, to hire journalists from favored associates of the ruling party, is a characteristic of an unfree press—a press whose journalists must be officially approved. Option D, to champion government platforms, is a common characteristic of an unfree press that is officially sanctioned by a ruling party. Of these answer choices, only option A describes behavior not associated with the official press in an authoritarian society. Thus, option A is the best answer choice.

Copyright © Mometrix Media. You have been licensed one copy of this document for personal use only. Any other reproduction or redistribution is strictly prohibited. All rights reserved.
This content is provided for test preparation purposes only and does not imply an endorsement by Mometrix of any particular political, scientific, or religious point of view.

5. D: The question here is asking about how a message is received by media consumers when it is presented in different media. Option A, the McCarthy hearings, mentions that the hearings were presented in two different media but does not illustrate a message being received differently by those two audiences. Option B, the statistic showing that more Americans vote in televised talent shows than for President, does not mention different types of media but merely different types of voting behaviors. Option C, the report on the decline of book sales, does mention two different media, books, and the internet, but does not provide an example of a message being received differently through those two media. Option D, the 1960 presidential debate, provides a clear example of two audiences consuming the same event through different media but interpreting its outcome differently. Option D is the best answer choice.

6. B: The Spanish-American War coincided with the beginning of the first tabloid media industry in America. "Yellow journalists" exaggerated or invented sensationalist stories to attract a larger audience and boost newspaper sales. Option A, to have students read stories by journalists of different nationalities, does not illustrate the issue of the tabloid media. Option B, to have students read factual and tabloid accounts of the event, would successfully illustrate this new role. Option C, to compare a contemporary article about the event with a later historical analysis of the war, would not help students to understand the role of the tabloid media. Option D, to explain the president's authority to control editorial content, is untrue and irrelevant to the subject of the tabloid media. Thus, option B is the best answer choice.

7. A: Option A, that the case allowed school authorities to censor student publications, is correct. The case ruled that school authorities could impose restrictions on freedom of speech if they had a valid educational reason to do so. Option B, that the case defended the right of school newspapers to enjoy the absolute protection of the First Amendment, is incorrect. An absolute right to free speech has not been legally established. Option C, that the case declared school newspapers exempt from libel laws, is inaccurate; libel laws apply to minors as well as to adults. Option D, that the case affirmed that underground student publications are not granted the same First Amendment protections as an official school newspaper, is untrue; in fact, the case declared that official school newspapers were more subject to official oversight by virtue of their status as official. Thus, option A is the best answer choice.

8. C: The press has many long-established roles: to inform, to persuade, and to entertain among others. Option A, a set of point-counterpoint columns, represents an attempt to provide balanced views rather than an attempt to influence public opinion. Option B, the publication of survey results, simply presents information without establishing an opinion. Option C, an editorial, represents an official opinion by the newspaper and an attempt to persuade the public to share it. Option D, a lead news story, may still be objective despite quoting opinionated individuals. A lead news story may present several opinions held by others without being seen as representing an official opinion of the paper itself. Option C, an editorial, is the best answer choice.

9. D: The key here is to identify a detail that distorts the central message of a story when included. Option A, a profile of a local politician, includes a detail about his differences with friends that add context and depth to his hobby. Option B, a feature story that quotes a business owner admitting to a crime, includes a detail that may have significance given the owner's political aspirations and so may be appropriate to include. Option C, a profile of business leaders, provides a political context and background for a human-interest profile. Option D, however, includes a piece of information that is irrelevant to the news issue being reported and characterizes the local citizen negatively. This inclusion leaves the paper open to charges of bias and lack of objectivity. Thus, option D is the best answer choice.

Copyright © Mometrix Media. You have been licensed one copy of this document for personal use only. Any other reproduction or redistribution is strictly prohibited. All rights reserved.
This content is provided for test preparation purposes only and does not imply an endorsement by Mometrix of any particular political, scientific, or religious point of view.

10. A: Option A, that private businesses purchase commercial airtime that funds television programs, is true. Television programs rely on funding from commercials and so risk alienating their sponsors with controversial content. Option B, that federal laws require equal airtime for political candidates, is true but irrelevant. This is not a good example of business interests influencing news content. Option C, that unions may have official opinions on public issues, may be true, but unions do not directly influence the content of news stories through their members. Option D, that a company has the right to challenge criticism on-air, is untrue. Thus, option A is the best answer choice.

11. B: Online media outlets are diverse in content and format, and there are few standards that can be universally applied to all of them. Option A, that online journalism has a stricter standard of fairness than print journalism does, is untrue. Online media outlets are diverse and unregulated and do not have a universally established tradition of peer review or fact checking. Option B, that stories published online can be posted and corrected quickly, is true. The speed and convenience of online media is one of its main advantages. Option C, that ownership of online media outlets is transparent, is untrue. Unlike print outlets, online outlets are not required to publish a statement of ownership or revenue. Option D, that the reliance of online media on advertising revenue makes it more responsive to readers, is a tenuous claim. Option B is the best answer choice.

12. A: The correct answer choice will contain an example supporting the student's thesis. Option A, that cable news networks have increased coverage of government, would seem to support it; cable news networks embody the traditional role of the press as a watchdog of government. Option B, that visual effects technology makes it more difficult to trust video footage produced by amateurs, does not support the idea of technology making society more democratic. Option C, that only qualified broadcast journalists have access to quality production equipment, is a dubious claim and, if true, does not support the idea of government responsiveness. Option D, that news networks may not project a presidential winner, is irrelevant to the question of technology. Thus, option A is the best answer choice.

13. A: The question asks about the role of the amateur in the production of television news. Option A, footage shot submitted by a viewer and used in a news program, is an example of the kind of video in question. Option B, footage of viewers discussing their tastes in news, does not address the issue of production. Option C, an interview with a former factory employee, involves a non-professional, but not in a production capacity. Option D, a news story aired on both television and the network's website, does not address the question at all. Therefore, option A is the best answer choice.

14. D: Option A, that television programs with low budgets receive a greater percentage of revenue from advertising, is not necessarily true, although it is possible that a low-budget program receives less overall revenue. Option B, that public television receives all of its funding from government and therefore cannot be considered objective, is untrue; public television receives funding from the government, but from other sources as well. Option C, that television is more responsive to viewer input because it is expensive to produce, is not necessarily true; in fact, expensive television often has a large audience, which would make it less likely to be responsive to any individual viewer's input. Option D, that all media relies on funding to be produced, is true. Both commercial and nonprofit media must rely on funding from advertising, government or private grants, or individuals to be produced. Therefore, option D is the best answer choice.

15. B: Option A, that media companies are primarily investment vehicles for their shareholders, is untrue. Media companies must, like any other companies, remain solvent but are not primarily investments. Option B, that media companies may have investments that create conflicts of interest,

Copyright © Mometrix Media. You have been licensed one copy of this document for personal use only. Any other reproduction or redistribution is strictly prohibited. All rights reserved.
This content is provided for test preparation purposes only and does not imply an endorsement by Mometrix of any particular political, scientific, or religious point of view.

is true. Media companies may own or be owned by other companies that prevent the objective reporting of stories about those companies. Option C, that media companies are nonprofit and subject to publishing rules, is not true. Other than standard libel laws, news organizations are not bound by law to publish or not publish anything. Option D, that newspapers are not allowed to publish stories about subjects related to their own business, is not true. Newspapers and television companies are not taxed differently, and while conflicts of interest may prevent the stories' objectivity, no laws prevent newspapers from publishing them. Therefore, option B is the best answer choice.

16. B: Option A, that the website is required to register its information with a national database, is untrue. No database of that kind exists. Option B, that a website where all articles are written by the same person is not subject to scrutiny over its stories, is a good choice. Caution should be exercised when using this website as a source. Option C, that the website is clearly a subjective source of information, is not necessarily true. While a journalist would be more careful in her use of this source, there may be value in this source if used correctly. Option D, that the website is probably reliable because online journalists must demonstrate professional credibility, is untrue. There are no specific professional requirements for starting a website and no rules governing the reliability of the information presented there. Therefore, option B is the best answer choice.

17. B: Option A, a basketball player who claims to use a pain reliever, is not a good fit. The player is not claiming a specific authority about the product but simply saying that he uses it. Option B, a commercial for cold medicine narrated by a man in a doctor's coat, is a good answer choice. Viewers do not know that the man is in fact a doctor; they only know that he is wearing a doctor's clothing. Option C, a commercial for a toy showing footage of children playing happily with it, does not suggest any kind of professional authority. Option D, a commercial for a prepared food with consumer testimonials, does not claim professional authority; in fact, it claims the authority of "real people" using the product and liking it. Only option B offers a suggestion of professional authority that remains unproven. Therefore, option B is the best answer.

18. C: Option A, superimposing a wide shot of a marching band with a close-up of the drum major, is not an ethical violation. The physical impossibility of the scene being taken in one photograph makes it obvious that the photo does not constitute trickery or manipulation. Option B, asking a student posing with a trophy to change his position, is also not a violation. It is an obviously posed photograph, rather than a candid one, and does not constitute an ethical violation. Option C, digitally removing a student from a group photograph, is an ethical violation. Even with permission from all the subjects, the photograph misrepresents reality. Option D, photographing the principal in a parking lot without explicit permission, is not a violation. Photographs can be taken in public settings without permission. Therefore, option C is the best answer choice.

19. B: Option A, a photo of a student fistfight in a parking lot after a football game, is ethical. Students have no reasonable expectation of privacy when in a public setting. Option B, an article mentioning the pregnancy of an abstinence-only sex education advocate, violates the privacy rights of the teenager and is unethical to print. Option C, a chart showing the total number of student arrests, is ethical. If no names are mentioned, there is no reason why a journalist should be prevented from analyzing the available data. Option D, an interview with a friend of a deceased student, is not an ethical violation, though it should be handled with care to avoid being tasteless. Option B is the best answer choice.

20. D: Option A, that students have no constitutionally protected right to free speech, is not true. Hazelwood v. Kuhlmeier limited freedom of speech in schools but did not establish that students have no right to free speech. Option B, that students have no protected right to publish particular

Copyright © Mometrix Media. You have been licensed one copy of this document for personal use only. Any other reproduction or redistribution is strictly prohibited. All rights reserved.
This content is provided for test preparation purposes only and does not imply an endorsement by Mometrix of any particular political, scientific, or religious point of view.

material, has been established, but not by Tinker. Option C, that the First Amendment applies no differently in public schools than elsewhere in society, is not true; limits can be placed on student speech by administrators if they have a "valid educational reason" for doing so according to several cases. Option D, that administrators must demonstrate a Constitutionally valid reason to regulate student speech, is true. Tinker established that students "are possessed of fundamental rights which the State must respect" and that can only be regulated with legitimate educational purpose. Therefore, option D is the best answer choice.

21. B: Prior restraint is the act of an outside source demanding control over whether a publication goes to print. Option A, an advisor asking for a story not to be printed based on its being possibly libelous, is not prior restraint; the advisor is acting in her official role in preventing the publication from being sued. Option B, a school administration demanding that controversial content not be printed, is a good choice. This practice is unacceptable and poor journalistic ethics. Option C, the subject of an article suing for the publication of non-factual information, is not correct. This is a legitimate response to the publication of libelous material. Option D, a school administration punishing a student for publishing profanity, is not prior restraint. Prior restraint relates to the authority to prevent publication, not to the punishment of an individual journalist. Therefore, option B is the best answer.

22. A: Online journalists are required to conform to all journalistic ethics, but the laws applying to them are slightly less restrictive than they are for print journalists. Option A, the responsibility to identify paid articles, does not apply to online journalists. Provided their information is factual, online journalists are free to publish whatever they see fit. Option B, the responsibility to credit all sources published elsewhere originally, is a responsibility incumbent upon all journalists, no matter their outlet. Option C, a responsibility to conform to libel laws, does in, fact, apply to online journalism as it applies to journalists elsewhere. Option D, a responsibility to protect sources who wish to remain anonymous, does apply to online journalists. Therefore, option A is the best choice.

23. C: It is important to maintain a publication free from conflict of interest. Option A, to assign the story to a student with no relationship to any party in the story, may be unrealistic, especially for a student publication. Reporters often have ongoing journalistic relationships with their subjects but must be careful to avoid bias in their writing. Option B, to run an editorial pointing out that the student should be given the benefit of the doubt, is unnecessary; a well-written article should make this point redundant. Option C, that the reporter should interview many and diverse sources, is a good way to ensure the reporting remains neutral. Option D, that the story should be cancelled, is unnecessary. Journalism often involves ongoing relationships, but the writer should take pains to remain unbiased in his writing. Therefore, option C is the best choice.

24. D: Journalists must ensure that their writing remains free from any accusations of ethical violations. Option A, opinions from students who believe that drugs should be legalized, may prove irrelevant to the article, but is not unethical to include them. Option B, quotations from students present during the incident, would be appropriate and ethical to include in an article of this nature. Option C, statistics about drug consumption among current students, would not be unethical to include but must be handled carefully to avoid endangering any of the survey participants. Option D, an interview with the student's doctor, is unethical to include. The student has an expectation of privacy in dealings with his or her physician, and in the unlikely event that the doctor is unethical enough to violate this privilege, the journalist is not excused from her obligations to remain ethical herself. Therefore, option D is the best choice.

25. D: Journalists must use resources in information gathering that are appropriate and specific to the scope of the article being researched. Option A, the website of the Texas Educational Authority,

Copyright © Mometrix Media. You have been licensed one copy of this document for personal use only. Any other reproduction or redistribution is strictly prohibited. All rights reserved.
This content is provided for test preparation purposes only and does not imply an endorsement by Mometrix of any particular political, scientific, or religious point of view.

would not be a good choice for a journalist researching comparative information among all 50 states. Option B, a chart from the United Nations educational organization, is unlikely to break statistics down within the United States in the way the journalist seeks. Option C, an interview with the school district superintendent, would not be helpful for someone looking for hard numbers. Option D, however, a database from the Department of Education, would be likely to include statistics on a national level and would be a good place for a journalist to start her research. Option D, therefore, is the best choice.

26. A: A journalist must ensure that the information on which her article relies is itself reputable. Option A, the fact that the article appears on a sports-equipment company's website, leaves the information open to accusations of bias, and therefore, it should not be used. Option B, that the article's author is a former professional athlete, does not prevent it from being used. The journalist, however, should make sure the article is legitimate and not a paid endorsement of a product. Option C, that the article focuses on only one brand of equipment, is acceptable, though the journalist should make sure her article includes other sources of information as well. Option D, that the article includes personal testimonials rather than scientific evidence, is not necessarily a problem, though it might be in a scientific publication. For a report of this nature, it is acceptable. Therefore, option A is the best choice.

27. C: A newspaper should be a holistic representation of the real makeup of the community. Option A, to publish the letter and a rebuttal, sets a tone of argumentation that does not fix the real problem of under-representation. Option B, to set a quota for minority representation, is a rigid response that fails to broaden the paper's coverage generally. Option C, to set a new policy of covering more sports, is a good response; it broadens the coverage without setting quotas that might make more diverse coverage a source of resentment. Option D, to ban the coverage of tennis, does not represent a holistic response to the problem. If the tennis team is having a winning season, then it should be covered. However, as a matter of general policy, the staff should ensure it broadens its coverage from now on. Therefore, option C is the best choice.

28. D: The student should consider the nature of the event when planning his reporting. Option A, to take a tape recorder, may be useful, but the Senator's answers are not likely to be long at a press conference. The student reporter will be lucky to have a single question answered and certainly should not expect long answers. Option B, to practice active listening skills that will make the Senator more comfortable, is irrelevant in a large and frantic press conference. Option C, to ask multi-part questions, is also impractical at a press conference. Reporters rarely get to ask extensive questions at an event like this. Option D, to plan several questions to ask and prioritize them, will allow the reporter to increase his chances of getting an answer to the question he finds most important. Option D, therefore, is the best choice.

29. C: Any source of information that has a personal author needs to be attributed to that author. Option A, a quotation from a public figure, needs to be attributed. There are different rules governing journalists' treatment of public figures versus private citizens, but attribution is not one of these differences. Option B, criticism by the principal, must be attributed as well. Option C, government statistics, should have their source cited, but do not need to be attributed to a personal author. Option D, a quotation from a famous poem, should be attributed to the author even if the author and poem are well-known. Option C, therefore, is the best choice.

30. A: A reporter must edit his story evenly without allowing the appearance of bias. Option A, that several points of view should remain represented but that they should not be redundant, is a good strategy. If two people share similar opinions on a subject, one of them can be cut from the article without sacrificing the representation of that opinion. Option B, that more quotations from people

Copyright © Mometrix Media. You have been licensed one copy of this document for personal use only. Any other reproduction or redistribution is strictly prohibited. All rights reserved.
This content is provided for test preparation purposes only and does not imply an endorsement by Mometrix of any particular political, scientific, or religious point of view.

who agree with the reporter should remain, is inappropriate. The reporter should have no point of view in the article in the first place. Option C, that only student voices should be represented, is not necessarily appropriate. Other sources of opinion may be of interest to students, even if students represent the bulk of the audience. Option D, that sources should be cut at random to ensure neutrality, is not a thoughtful method for cutting a story. Therefore, option A is the best choice.

31. B: Unbiased reporting should emphasize a variety of points of view. Option A, having students assume different voices in their writing, is not helpful to learning about information gathering. Option B, to list potentially useful interviewees for an article, is useful in helping students to think about broadening their interview sources. Option C, an outlining assignment assessing the flow of information in a story, is not helpful in learning about interviewing. Option D, a paired assignment in interviewing, does not get students to think about a variety of interview sources but merely about to ask questions of a particular person. Option B, therefore, is the best answer choice.

32. C: Option A, an unbiased account of facts, does not characterize an editorial. An editorial's purpose is to represent a particular persuasive argument. Option B, the point of view of one identified writer, describes an op-ed piece, not an editorial. Both forms of writing, however, do represent opinion. Option C, the official opinion of the entire newspaper staff, does describe an editorial. An editorial represents the unified point of view of the paper itself. Option D, factually based but not as timely as a news story, is an inaccurate description of an editorial. An editorial, again, is an official opinion, not a factual account. Option C, therefore, is the best answer choice.

33. D: Any given publication should address issues that affect and are of interest to its core readership. Option A, a feature story on college scholarships for student athletes, does this; it is of interest to at least some of a readership composed of high school students. Option B, a news story on the school football team's winning season, is also of interest to a student population. Option C, an investigation into funding discrepancies affecting various local football programs, is also at least potentially of interest to high school students. An article does not have to report only on the activities that go on inside school walls to be of interest to that school's population. Option D, a report on a new local professional football team, is not an appropriate article for a school newspaper. This subject would be better covered by a city newspaper. Option D, therefore, is the best answer.

34. C: Student involvement in extracurricular activities should remain the focus of this article. Option A, a photo of a student pilot, is well within the scope of this article. Option B, a quotation from a student resentful that school pulls him away from his athletic goals, is appropriate as well; though it's a negative opinion, it still addresses aspects of the article's purpose. Option C, a quotation from a teacher about extracurricular funding, is not really within the purview of this article, which is about participation in activities, not funding of them. Option D, a complaint about students who participate in these activities, is a negative opinion, but still very much related to the scope of the article as it focuses on participation. Option C, therefore, is the best answer choice.

35. A: Attribution must be provided for all sources of quotations in an article. Option A, a spokesperson who provided only statistics, is a good answer choice. Statistics do not need attribution to a person, especially if they are publicly available. Option B, an exchange student quoted on her experiences, needs attribution as would any quote. Option C, a student who wishes to remain anonymous, still needs attribution, though that attribution can come in the form of "said a student who wished to remain anonymous." Option D, the school principal, must be attributed. All sources of direct quotations must be acknowledged whether they are well-known or wish not to have their names used. Option A, therefore, is the best answer choice.

Copyright © Mometrix Media. You have been licensed one copy of this document for personal use only. Any other reproduction or redistribution is strictly prohibited. All rights reserved.
This content is provided for test preparation purposes only and does not imply an endorsement by Mometrix of any particular political, scientific, or religious point of view.

36. B: A photo caption should add relevant information but remain within the scope of the article to which it is attached. Option A, a description of the photographed action and additional information about the subject, is not a good choice unless the article is a feature about this particular student. Since it is a news story about the game, this is a poor choice. Option B, a description of the action and additional information about the story, is appropriate. Option C, a description of the photographed action, is not useful. It provides the reader with no information that they could not have gleaned for themselves. Option D, a description of the game's action, has no relationship to the photograph. A photograph's caption must tie together the information provided in the photograph and that given by the article. Option B, therefore, is the best answer choice.

37. B: A good exercise for students learning about the differences among types of journalistic writing should incorporate examples of the different types. Option A, having them write an article and then using it in a broadcast exercise, does not help to clarify the differences for them. Option B, providing a list of published or broadcast sentences and having students assign them to a category, would be a useful exercise. Professional examples of proper style would better illustrate the differences in styles than would having students try to create the differences themselves. Option C, having students copyedit articles for different formats, would not teach them proper style. Option D, having students transcribe a broadcast story and apply print journalism rules to it, is irrelevant. Of the above choices, only option B provides students with clear examples of proper journalistic writing. Therefore, option B is the best choice.

38. D: Option A, reorganizing the story in chronological order, is inappropriate journalistic writing and would not necessarily result in the desired quote being moved up in the story. Option B, to accept that it must be cut off, is not appropriate. If the student feels that the quotation is relevant, then the problem is that it should be moved up in the story to have more importance. Option C, to include the quotation in an earlier paragraph with another quotation, is inappropriate. Quotations should always be one per paragraph. Option D, to edit the lead, may be the best course of action. If a student is finding that a useful quote falls too far down in the story, then perhaps the lead isn't properly communicating what is important in the story. Option D, therefore, is the best answer choice.

39. A: Two-line headlines should be clear, easy to read, and unambiguous. Option A, to avoid awkward line breaks, helps students to maintain clarity in headline writing. Option B, to avoid direct quotations, does not help make headlines clear. Direct quotations, if incorporated elegantly, can be used in headlines to great effect. Option C, to avoid using more than one subject and verb, is not necessarily helpful. Headlines using more than one subject and verb must be carefully constructed to be easy to read, but there is no reason they should be avoided on principle. Option D, to keep all subjects on the same line, often compounds awkwardness. It is usually more elegant to split up subjects in a two-line headline. Option A, therefore, is the best answer choice.

40. C: A staff stylebook is helpful for journalists who have local issues to address in writing that are not necessarily covered by the AP stylebook. Option A, a student who does not know what to cut from a story, will not be served by a staff stylebook. Option B, a student with a question about federal obscenity rules, would be better off seeking legal advice than turning to a stylebook. Option C, a student figuring out how to attribute a quote to Dr. Smith, should be able to look in a stylebook for this answer. Option D, a student seeking help with ad placement, would not be served by a stylebook. Option C, therefore, is the best answer choice.

41. D: If the article is too long but the sentence count is low, the sentences are likely too long. Option A, using shorter words, will not improve the flow of the article since it does not create shorter sentences. Option B, removing entire paragraphs, may cut the article for length but will not

Copyright © Mometrix Media. You have been licensed one copy of this document for personal use only. Any other reproduction or redistribution is strictly prohibited. All rights reserved.
This content is provided for test preparation purposes only and does not imply an endorsement by Mometrix of any particular political, scientific, or religious point of view.

improve the sentences, which themselves need to be short and to the point. Option C, combining paragraphs, will probably make the problem worse; a reader will lose interest in an article that has only a few paragraphs full of long sentences. Option D, however, using active voice verbs and avoiding unnecessary words, will tighten the story's word count, resulting in shorter sentences and a better overall flow without sacrificing information. Option D, therefore, is the best answer choice.

42. A: The pitfall in having a student journalist report on a subject about which he is familiar is that he may assume the audience is as familiar with the subject as he is himself. Option A, to avoid jargon unfamiliar to a reader, is a good choice. This will enable the article to hold the interest of a reader, even one who doesn't already know about the subject. Option B, to warm the audience that the article contains unfamiliar words, will likely alienate the uninformed reader. Option C, to keep the article short, will not help the writer interest a reader who is unfamiliar with the language of the subject. Option D, to write in the passive voice, is bad advice for any article. Sentences should remain short, informative, and active. Option A, therefore, is the best answer choice.

43. B: Inspiring journalism students with renowned articles from history is always a good object lesson. Option A, to better understand the differing ethical standards of one historical period versus the current period, is inaccurate; ethical standards for journalists are basically consistent, though the specific technical challenges have evolved in recent decades. Option B, to appreciate the development of journalistic standards through the ages, is a good description of this exercise's value. Option C, to appreciate how online culture has influenced writing practices recently, does not help to explain the value of reading older articles. Option D, to distinguish between older, personal essays and recent, fact-based articles, is inaccurate. News writing has always been based on fact; it was not an invention of recent years. Option B, therefore, is the best answer choice.

44. D: Option A, the increased use of color photography, has not changed the basic issues of copyright infringement. Option B, the development of centralized wire services, has nothing at all to do with copyright issues. Option C, the use of word processors, is a development of recent decades but not one that has created challenges in the area of copyright protection. Option D, the introduction of digital files for photographic work, has had an effect on copyright; because digital files are consistent even when copied, they are easier to transmit and manipulate, creating problems in copyright enforcement. Option D, therefore, is the best answer choice.

45. C: Which of the above categories, if any, are treated differently from ordinary private citizens when it comes to privacy expectations? Option A, that there are no exceptions, is not true; there are categories that are treated differently than others legally. Option B, with the exception of foreign nationals, is not true; citizenship has no effect on privacy expectations. Option C, with the exception of public figures and celebrities, is true; politicians and others whose lives are lived largely in public have a diminished legal expectation of privacy compared to others. Option D, that privacy expectations apply only to adults, is not true; all private citizens, adult or not, have protected privacy status. Option C, therefore, is the best answer choice.

46. C: Different shooting situations call for different photographic lenses. Option A, a macro lens, is not appropriate for a soccer game. A macro lens is typically used in an extreme close-up shooting situation. Option B, a fisheye lens, is inappropriate as well for a soccer game since it actually distorts the image it captures. Option C, a telephoto lens, would be appropriate in a sports situation; telephoto lenses capture images from great distances. Option D, a shift-control lens, would not apply in this situation. Shift-control lenses are typically used to maintain an upright shooting position even when shooting something very tall, such as a building. Option C, therefore, is the best answer choice.

Copyright © Mometrix Media. You have been licensed one copy of this document for personal use only. Any other reproduction or redistribution is strictly prohibited. All rights reserved.
This content is provided for test preparation purposes only and does not imply an endorsement by Mometrix of any particular political, scientific, or religious point of view.

47. A: Option A, that they should tie the information in the photo to the information in the article, is accurate; a photo caption could, for instance, point out the individual in a group photo who is discussed in the article, putting him in context. Option B, that captions should describe the action in the photo, is not a good goal for a caption; this would add nothing to the information the reader has already received simply by looking at the photo. Option C, that the caption should list the individuals in the photo, is not the whole story; a good caption will also point out further information, adding to the story. Option D, that it should reproduce the main thrust of the article's lead paragraph, is not accurate. Photo captions should always aim to provide readers with additional information. Option A, therefore, is the best answer choice.

48. B: The goal of representing a population holistically is a tricky one; coverage should represent the real diversity of the population without sacrificing the criterion of newsworthiness. Option A, to create a checklist of minority groups, is not a good strategy. This quota may result in each group being represented only once rather than achieving the better goal of holistically representing the student body. Option B, including many students in photographic coverage, is a more flexible goal that is more likely to result in successfully authentic coverage. Option C, to avoid individual photographs, is counterproductive; photographers should be free of restrictive constraints such as this one. Option D, to ensure the staff is diverse, is itself a good aim, but to divide the staff among demographic lines in their reporting assignments will result in a more, not less, divided student community. Option B, therefore, is the best answer choice.

49. D: The rule of thirds applies to the composition of photographs, and its use distinguishes a good photograph from a bad one. Option A, the relationship of the f-stop with increased distance from the subject, is not accurate; f-stops are related to the amount of light let into the camera, not distance from the subject. Option B, the amount of light registered on film, is not accurate either. Option C, the relationship between shutter speed and the f-stop, is not this simple; photographers have a great deal of freedom to adjust both these variables for different effects. Option D, the alignment of important compositional elements, does accurately describe the rule of thirds. Option D, therefore, is the best answer choice.

50. C: A shallow depth of field means that only a very narrow band will be in focus in the photograph. Option A, to use shallow depth of field when photographing a subject far away, is not a good plan; nearly the entire photograph will be out of focus. Option B, to use it to photograph a subject in motion, is not how shallow depth of field is typically used. Option C, to use it to isolate an important element from the background, is a much better use of shallow depth of field. Option D, to photograph several objects at several distances with shallow depth of field, is wrong; this is precisely the situation when one would want to avoid a shallow depth of field. Option C, therefore, is the best answer choice.

51. A: To ensure the photograph suits as many potential purposes as possible, the student should scan the photograph in such a way that he is able to maintain much of its quality. Option A, to scan the photograph at high resolution, would accomplish this. Option B, to crop the photograph, is a bad strategy, as it is an action that cannot be undone, and the student may later discover that he wishes to use part of the photograph that he had deleted. Option C, to desaturate the image, is another action that cannot be undone and so is a bad idea. Option D, to shrink the photograph, is a bad strategy; if the student later wishes to use the photograph at its original size, it will have lost quality when he tries to enlarge it. Option A, therefore, is the best answer choice.

52. C: Leading lines are an important principle in photography. Option A, the imaginary lines that divide a photograph into nine equal rectangles, relates to the rule of thirds, not to leading lines. Option B, the line of code that contains information about a digital image, is not an accurate

Copyright © Mometrix Media. You have been licensed one copy of this document for personal use only. Any other reproduction or redistribution is strictly prohibited. All rights reserved.
This content is provided for test preparation purposes only and does not imply an endorsement by Mometrix of any particular political, scientific, or religious point of view.

description of leading lines. Option C, a compositional line directing the eye to the main subject, does accurately describe leading lines. Option D, the imaginary lines marking off the outer 10% of a photograph that will not be visible in a printed newspaper, is not accurate. There is no loss of image in a printed newspaper in the way this answer choice describes. Option C, therefore, is the best answer choice.

53. A: A photo essay should contain photographs that are compelling, tell a story, and interest the reader. Option A, a posed headshot of the band leader, is not a compelling photograph. It does not add information to a story. Option B, a close up of instruments, adds interest and information to the story being told. Option C, an action shot of a trombonist, certainly adds interest. Option D, a candid shot of three musicians resting, helps to add information to the story being told. Of the above choices, only option A sounds like it would not add interest to the photo essay. Therefore, option A is the best answer choice.

54. B: Given the constraints imposed on the paper, the goal should be to make the paper look professional without drawing attention to its meager page count. Option A, to divide the paper into three sections with unique looks and layouts, would only serve to draw the reader's attention to the small size of each section. Option B, to limit the number of styles used throughout the paper, would make the paper look cohesive and distinctive, without subdividing it into several paltry sections. Option C, to place many stories on the front page, with jumps to later pages, would make many of the latter pages look unprofessional and sloppy. Option D, to decrease the size of headlines and photos, would fail to break up the space of the page in a meaningful way. Only option B would improve the look of the paper; therefore, option B is the best answer choice.

55. C: The described layout can only be meaningfully used in particular kinds of publications. Option A, a student art publication, would be ill-served by this kind of layout. An art publication should devote a relatively high amount of space to each featured artwork rather than crowding them together. Option B, a literary magazine, would not need to feature so many photographs, and the text should be the focus of the page rather than an afterthought featured on the margins. Option C, a yearbook, would be well-suited to this design; photographs feature prominently in yearbooks, and there are often many of them. Option D, a broadsheet newspaper, would also have text as the dominant feature rather than a secondary consideration. Option C, therefore, is the best answer choice.

56. B: Option A, to switch the placement of article E and photo B, would result in two similarly sized headlines (on articles A and E), creating visual confusion. Option B, to move article C up on the page and move article A and photo B down on the page, would be a good strategy. Article C, being longer and with a larger headline, seems like it would be well suited to more prominent placement on the page. Option C, to eliminate photo B and spread article A over three columns, would result in an already relatively short article taking up even less vertical room on the page and would likely make the page look unbalanced. Option D, to move article E to another page and replace it with a photo, would create a dominance of photos rather than text on the page. Option B, therefore, is the best answer choice.

57. A: It is important to represent data with the most appropriate type of visual. Option A, a pie chart, would be a good use of this data; there will likely only be a few broad categories of data to represent, and a reader can tell at a glance which categories are bigger and which smaller. Option B, a bar graph, is good at showing the size of categories but would not be as good as a pie chart in showing what percentage of the whole population each category represents. Option C, a pictogram, would not be the best choice here; pictograms use art to illustrate the sizes of categories within a chart, and it is not immediately obvious that artwork is what is needed here. Option D, a line graph,

Copyright © Mometrix Media. You have been licensed one copy of this document for personal use only. Any other reproduction or redistribution is strictly prohibited. All rights reserved.
This content is provided for test preparation purposes only and does not imply an endorsement by Mometrix of any particular political, scientific, or religious point of view.

typically shows how a number changes over time, which is not the data being represented. Option A, therefore, is the best choice.

58. A: Particular rules apply to two-page spreads in order to keep the visual elements in proper relationship and avoid confusing any readers. Option A, the headline at the top, is a problem. Headlines should never cross gutters. Option B, the small article at the left, is not a problem. In a yearbook spread, text is often placed at the outer margins of a spread since photographs are dominant. Option C, the small photo on the left page, is fine as well. Photos are typically placed on the inner margins of a yearbook spread, and two identically-sized smaller photos on the left contrasted with a large photo on the right creates a good visual balance. Option D, the large photo on the right, is well placed on the page and does not create any design problems. Option A is the element most in need of improvement and is, therefore, the best choice.

59. D: Option A, to use desktop publishing software to design graphics and artwork, is not the best use of this software, which is typically used to arrange elements on a page once they have been created. Option B, to write the text of the articles, is a task best suited to word-processing software where functions such as spell check can be employed. Option C, adjusting the color and cropping photos, is best done in a graphics program rather than desktop publishing software. Option D, arranging the stories, photos, and masthead on the page, is what desktop publishing software was designed to do. Option D, therefore, is the best answer choice.

60. C: The significance of photojournalists like Dorothea Lange rested in the way they exposed a nation of readers to the photographic reality of the Great Depression. Option A, that they inspired President Roosevelt's New Deal programs, is incorrect; in fact, photojournalists like Lange were employed by Roosevelt's programs. Option B, that they were the first nationally-published documentary photography, is inaccurate. These photojournalists were significant, but they were not the first photojournalists. Option C, that they published the reality of economic desperation, is true; for the first time, readers around the United States saw the effects of the Depression around the country. Option D, that they were the first published works by women photojournalists, is not true. Dorothea Lange was a significant female photojournalist but not the first one in history. Option C, therefore, is the best answer choice.

61. A: It is important to maintain a balanced look for any given page of a newspaper. Option A, to support one of the stories with a photo, would help add visual interest to this page. Option B, to increase the size of the advertisement, would be impractical and would set an unfair precedent since the advertiser has paid only for the smaller size. Option C, to add length to each of the articles, would require additional work from each of the writers of the four articles, and there may not be the material to support it. Option D, to increase the size of the smallest headline, is probably a poor idea since it may result in the headline being disproportionately large compared to the article. Therefore, option A is the best answer choice.

62. D: The dynamics of a color photograph are different from those of a black-and-white photograph and should be adjusted carefully for reproduction. Option A, solarization, is a visual effect resulting from over-exposure of a film negative and would not be an appropriate adjustment. Option B, cropping, is a process of selecting certain parts of the image for reproduction. Option C, file format conversion, affects the way the image is stored digitally but does not affect the color in a substantial way. Option D, however, saturation and contrast, makes adjustments to the amount of color in a photograph and would be an appropriate adjustment to make. Therefore, option D is the best answer choice.

Copyright © Mometrix Media. You have been licensed one copy of this document for personal use only. Any other reproduction or redistribution is strictly prohibited. All rights reserved.
This content is provided for test preparation purposes only and does not imply an endorsement by Mometrix of any particular political, scientific, or religious point of view.

63. B: The front page of a newspaper establishes the tone for the issue, and should be treated carefully. Option A, to maximize the number of photos on the front page, is not a universal rule. The number of photos on the front page should be evaluated on a case-by-case basis. Option B, never to run an advertisement on the front page, is true. Front pages are considered too important to include advertising. Option C, that there should be at least 10 stories on a front page, is inaccurate. While this may have been the case in previous decades, the number is now typically closer to five. Option D, that op-ed pieces should be featured at the bottom of the front page, is not true; op-ed pieces do not usually run on the front page at all. Option B is the best choice.

64. C: An effective ad should appeal directly to the newspaper's readership. Option A, a photograph of the owner, is not likely to have an effect on students. Option B, a freehand drawing of a cup of coffee, while better than no artwork, is not the best choice. Option C, a color photograph of a student at the coffee shop, will likely appeal to students who are likely to look at the ad and possibly recognize the student in the photo. Option D, a logo derived from a popular soft drink brand, is likely to be a violation of copyright and should not be used. Option C is the best answer choice.

65. D: A script font is difficult to read and should only be used as an accent in specific situation. Option A, in the nameplate for a student newspaper, is an inappropriate use of a script font. Option B, in a bar graph, is also inappropriate; bar graphs should be easy to read at a glance. Option C, within the body text in a yearbook spread, is a poor choice for a script font; script should never be used for body text. Option D, as the headline of a yearbook spread, would be an appropriate use for an unusual font. A yearbook page is casual and the headline is short enough that reading an unusual font would not be difficult. Therefore, option D is the best answer choice.

66. B: Although putting a print version of a newspaper online in this way seems like it would save time, there are a number of disadvantages. Option A, articles that continue on another page and are difficult to navigate, is one disadvantage. Option B, that uploading the data takes longer, is actually not true; it is faster, but it really isn't worth the effort to do it this way due to the other disadvantages it presents. Option C, that saving the articles as graphics files takes up more server space, is true. Option D, that the articles will not be scannable for keywords, is true; when the text is uploaded as a graphic, it will not be identifiable in searches. Therefore, option B is the only choice that is NOT a disadvantage and is, therefore, the best answer.

67. B: Generally, the development of cable television technology resulted in a broadening of available television programming in the US Option A, that television programming became privatized, is not true; American television has never been a public monopoly. Option B, that there was an increase in the number and specificity of television channels, did in fact result from the development of cable TV. Option C, that television programming was deregulated, is not true; the Federal Communications Commission still regulates television programming in the United States. Option D, that programming began to be broadcast 24 hours a day, did not result from the development of cable TV. Therefore, option B is the best answer choice.

68. A: President Roosevelt was among the first government officials to make use of radio technology. Option A, that he used radio to reach a national audience, accurately describes the significance of the Fireside Chats. Option B, that they passed encoded messages to counterespionage operatives, is untrue. Option C, that it was the first time a US president appeared on television, is not accurate; Roosevelt was the first American president on television, but the Fireside Chats were strictly a radio phenomenon. Option D, that they were the first successful use of mass media in a national election campaign, is not true; the Fireside Chats were not used as a campaign tool. Therefore, option A is the best answer choice.

Copyright © Mometrix Media. You have been licensed one copy of this document for personal use only. Any other reproduction or redistribution is strictly prohibited. All rights reserved.
This content is provided for test preparation purposes only and does not imply an endorsement by Mometrix of any particular political, scientific, or religious point of view.

69. C: One main difference between print and broadcast writing is that print can be read at a reader's pace rather than fitting into time constraints. Option A, that a print writer has less flexibility to use alliteration and poetic language, is not true, a print writer has more flexibility in this respect. Option B, that a print writer must avoid repetitive words, is not any truer for print writers than it is for broadcast writers. Option C, that a print writer can present information in a denser writing style is true. A reader confused by what they have read can re-read the sentence; this is not true for a viewer of broadcast news. Option D, that a writer for print must always use the present tense, is not true; both print and broadcast writers use whatever tense is appropriate to the situation. Therefore, option C is the best answer choice.

70. D: Option A, that viewers tend to pay more attention to news broadcasters with whom they can identify, is not an important factor in news writing. Option B, that the audio narrative must be able to stand on its own, is inaccurate; audio and video work together in a broadcast. Option C, that the primary function of a broadcast is to confirm community standards, is not accurate; the function of a news broadcast is to inform viewers about important events. Option D, that viewers have only one chance to register the information, is true. Broadcast writing must be simple and straightforward in order to communicate effectively the first time to viewers. Therefore, option D is the best answer choice.

71. A: The role of a news director relates to overseeing the general daily production of a broadcast. Option A, handles the details of camera placement and staff activities, accurately describes the scale of a director's activities. Option B, controls the on-air video switcher and technical equipment, applies more to a technical director than to a director whose job is less detail-oriented. Option C, reads recorded stories on-air and conducts interviews, is the description of a news anchor, not a director. Option D, compiles news stories from recorded videotape, describes the role of a news editor who creates the finished product of a story once the footage has been shot. Therefore, option A is the best answer choice.

72. B: B-roll is an important term to know when producing video reports. Option A, a fade to black between shots, is not accurate. A fade to black is technically a transition since it gets the viewer from one shot to the next. Option B, a silent shot of a shelf of bowling trophies, is a good example of b-roll. Shot footage that is not part of the interview but includes additional visual information that adds to the story is b-roll. Option C, a shot of the interview that includes both the student and his father, is not b-roll since the interviewer and interviewee are both on camera. Option D, a shot of the student alone asking questions, is also not b-roll since what we are viewing is the same as what we are seeing. Option B, therefore, is the best answer choice.

73. D: There are actually a few restrictions that apply to broadcast but not print media of which student journalists should be aware. Option A, that a specific number of stories can be presented in a broadcast, is inaccurate. Within the time frame booked for a broadcast any number of stories can be presented. Option B, that broadcast stories must be produced far in advance, is untrue; while some aspects of news production are produced in advance, they also cover developing news stories daily. Option C, that broadcast news must legally devote a percentage of its time to advertising, is untrue; broadcast news sells advertising but is not legally obligated to do so. Option D, that regulations restrict content for broadcast productions, is true: the FCC restricts language and content of broadcast media in a way that does not affect print media. Option D, then, is the right answer choice.

74. D: A transition is a video technique that is used between shots as a way to move from one shot to another and to give a certain mood to the video. Option A, that it should be used during the questions, is inappropriate and would be awkward. Option B, that it should be used during the

Copyright © Mometrix Media. You have been licensed one copy of this document for personal use only. Any other reproduction or redistribution is strictly prohibited. All rights reserved.
This content is provided for test preparation purposes only and does not imply an endorsement by Mometrix of any particular political, scientific, or religious point of view.

answers, suffers from the same problem of awkwardness. Option C, that it should be used between a wide shot and a close up of the same subject, could theoretically be used but would look strange since the basic content of the video frame does not change. Option D, between a shot of the friend and a shot of the friend's home, would be an ideal position for a transition: between two shots whose content is different. Option D, then, is the best answer choice.

75. A: It is important for students to be aware of the time restrictions and necessity of prioritizing stories in a news broadcast. Option A, that students can evaluate how stories are prioritized, is a good illustration of the purpose of this exercise. Option B, that students can analyze the advertising, is irrelevant; to time the stories and list their order would not reveal any insights about advertising. Option C, that the students can analyze the anchors' tone, again, would not be served by looking at the timing and order of the stories presented. Option D, that the students can analyze the elimination of stories, would not be served by this exercise. Students will have no way of knowing which stories were eliminated in order to present the ones shown. Therefore, option A is the best choice.

76. A: Although at first a contract rate may seem like a loss of revenue, it has compensations. Option A, that it will decrease the cost in acquisition time and energy per ad for the staff, is the major advantage. Option B, that the contract will allow the newspaper to run ultimately less advertising, is untrue; because the revenue per ad is decreased, theoretically the newspaper will have to run more advertising. Option C, that the appearance of corporate sponsorship will increase credibility, is untrue; a regular advertiser does not necessarily suggest corporate sponsorship, and if it did, it would decrease credibility. Option D, that it will enable the staff to track the effectiveness of advertising throughout the year, does not necessarily follow from a contract rate. Therefore, option A is the best answer choice.

77. B: It is important when soliciting advertising to make a case to the potential advertiser that your outlet will reach the appropriate audience. Option A, an advertisement the business has placed elsewhere, is not convincing on this point; a staffer should be familiar with the business, but it is more important to persuade the owner that one's own outlet is a good choice. Option B, statistics showing an increase in student business for businesses placing ads, would be a good choice that would show the owner this was a good strategy. Option C, a recent copy of the paper, will not convince the owner that they should place an ad. Option D, a receipt showing the number of copies produced, will not prove the suitability of the paper for this advertiser. Option B, therefore, is the best answer choice.

78. C: There are a few basic rules for good ads, and they are well worth knowing. Option C, making the type smaller, will not result in the ad drawing attention. It will result in the ad being ignored. Option B, adding contact information, is always important so that readers can locate the business. Option A, adding a graphic, will result in increased interest in the ad. Option D, printing it in color, will also make it more eye-catching. Of the above options, only option C will result in decreased interest in the advertisement. Therefore, option C is the best answer choice.

79. D: Never promise a business owner anything you cannot deliver. Option A, suggesting the business is popular with students, is a legitimate selling point. Option B, telling the owner that the staffer himself frequents her establishment, is legitimate, provided that it is true. Option C, offering a discount if the owner purchases an ad in every issue of the newspaper, is very commonly done. It is called a "contract rate." Option D, guaranteeing a 5% increase in business from students, is not ethical. The staffer has no way of being able to guarantee that will actually happen, and it is unethical to guarantee a return on investment. Option D, therefore, is the best answer choice.

Copyright © Mometrix Media. You have been licensed one copy of this document for personal use only. Any other reproduction or redistribution is strictly prohibited. All rights reserved.
This content is provided for test preparation purposes only and does not imply an endorsement by Mometrix of any particular political, scientific, or religious point of view.

80. C: Incorporating advertising into a yearbook in an organic way will increase reader interest in the ads and make the prospect of advertising more enticing to businesses. Option A, to incorporate ads into editorials endorsing the products, is unethical. Option B, to group all advertisements into their own section, will in fact make it easier for students to skip all the ads at once and never look at any of them. Option C, to place the ads on pages featuring candid photos, would be an excellent way to incorporate advertising since students will be more likely to look at those pages. Option D, to group all advertisements together in a stand-alone supplement to the yearbook, is the worst option. Students are likely to throw away the entire section and never open it if it is clearly marked as advertising. Option C, therefore, is the best answer choice.

81. D: Option A, when the business has artwork it wishes to incorporate, is not a good time to use a classified ad. Classified ads rarely incorporate artwork. Option B, when the business's advertising budget is large, is not appropriate either: a display ad is far more effective at catching a viewer's attention when a business has money to spend. Option C, when it wishes to attract the attention of a new audience, is also not a good situation to employ a classified ad; classified ads are rarely used by viewers who are simply browsing through the newspaper. Option D, when the potential audience is already seeking a particular product, is the best situation in which to purchase a classified ad. Ads are organized by type of product, making it easy for a viewer in the market for a product to find it. Option D, therefore, is the best answer choice.

82. A: The main purpose served by reaching out into the community would be to establish the school as a strong part of the community. Option A, that it would reinforce connections between students and the community, is another way of saying this. Option B, that it would broaden the audience for the advertisers, may be a side effect but is ultimately not the main purpose of doing this. Option C, that it would allow public input on the content of the paper, is not the purpose of distributing the paper in the community; ultimately the responsibility for the paper's content lies with the staff. Option D, that it would expose the writing of student journalists to a professional audience, is not the purpose. If students wish to have professionals read their work, there are more direct methods for accomplishing this. Option A, therefore, is the best answer choice.

83. C: The role of a student newspaper advisor is multifaceted and not easily pinned down. Option A, to exercise prior restraint over student writing, is not the role of a student advisor; students ultimately have editorial control over their own products. Option B, to select and assign articles to student journalists, describes the role of the managing editor, not the advisor. Option C, to educate students about the practice of journalism and consult on production problems, does describe the general role of an advisor. Option D, to copyedit articles and oversee photographic work, is the role that should be assigned to students, not to an adult advisor. Option C, therefore, is the best answer choice.

84. C: Keeping track of changes to layouts over time can be useful and time-saving for students. Option A, that it enables credit to be given for successful ideas, is not really the point. This notebook should show ideas evolving over time, so isolating successful ideas as the product of one person is not easy. Option B, that it encourages competition, is not the case. Quite the opposite: the notebook should encourage staffers to work together and learn from everyone's ideas, successful and unsuccessful. Option C, that it enables staff to track unsuccessful ideas, is true. This notebook should save time and energy should someone think about returning to an old idea at a later date. Option D, that it gives future staff a goal to which to aspire, is not the aim here. A notebook like this should be practically useful in the near term. Option C, therefore, is the best answer choice.

85. A: The purpose of peer review is to help students become aware of the many relationships necessary in producing quality journalism work. Option A, that students can learn that journalism is

Copyright © Mometrix Media. You have been licensed one copy of this document for personal use only. Any other reproduction or redistribution is strictly prohibited. All rights reserved.
This content is provided for test preparation purposes only and does not imply an endorsement by Mometrix of any particular political, scientific, or religious point of view.

a collaborative effort, says this nicely. Option B, that students will learn that the quality of their work will always be evaluated partly on preconceived notions, is not the aim here. Grading should be fair but should reflect all the ways in which a staffer improves the journalistic process. Option C, that students learn that the goal is to please as many people as possible, is untrue. Such an impossible goal would result in substandard journalism. Option D, that students learn that the opinions of readers are less important than those of journalists, is not true. Journalists have important relationships with many categories of people, all of which must be maintained. Option A, therefore, is the best answer choice.

86. B: Students often think of journalism as an individual pursuit, but group exercises are important in teaching collaboration. Option A, that students learn the value of healthy competition, is not the goal here. A successful editorial will be the product of collaboration, not competition. Option B, that students will learn to work collaboratively, describes the goal of the exercise well. Option C, that students will appreciate the freedom to work alone without obstruction, is not the purpose; there is value in learning to work in groups to create a strong editorial. Option D, that students will learn to choose writing partners who share their points of view, is not the purpose either. In an editorial, students should learn to ask each other valuable questions and respond to others' concerns not simply to locate staff members who agree with them. Option B, therefore, is the best answer choice.

87. D: A contest situation should be employed only when it results in a better journalistic product. Option A, to reward students for quality photographic work, is not an ideal situation; students are probably producing their best work already, and a contest will reward more talented students. Option B, to encourage students to come up with as many article topics as possible, is not likely to result in a better newspaper since the contest rewards quantity of ideas without considering quality. Option C, to reward students for improving their first drafts, only encourages students to do something they are likely to be doing anyway. Option D, to encourage the correction of typographical errors, is a good situation for a contest. At this publication stage, students often fail to take responsibility for the paper's quality, and a contest will encourage them to proofread carefully. Option D is the best answer choice.

88. B: Diversity is an important goal, but it should be achieved organically without creating additional problems. Option A, choosing a representative from each ethnic group, is a poor choice. It ignores the journalistic talent of individual minority staffers and instead, ghettoizes them as representatives of an ethnic group. Option B, compiling a list of weaknesses and identifying new staffers who could strengthen these areas, is a better strategy. A homogenous staff often fails to cover the school's diversity well enough, and identifying potential staffers who could help in problem areas allows them to be seen as contributing journalistic value rather than simply filling a quota. Option C, selecting candidates randomly, fails to take the selection process seriously. Option D, for the advisor to assume a main selection role, is irresponsible; students should take responsibility for the quality of their staff and their newspaper. Option B is the best answer choice.

89. A: An editorial should reflect the unified opinion of the staff as a whole. Option A, to ask the staff to write an alternative editorial and have the two disagreeing students do a point-counterpoint piece, solves the problem elegantly. Option B, to assign the writing of the editorial to the managing editor, ignores the spirit of editorial writing, which should representative the coherent vision of the staff. Option C, to ask the lowest-ranking staffer to recuse herself, again ignores the spirit of editorial writing and creates unnecessary divisions within the staff. Option D, to advise the staff to represent both points of view in the editorial, would result in a sloppy editorial that lacked a clear vision. Option A, therefore, is the best answer choice.

Copyright © Mometrix Media. You have been licensed one copy of this document for personal use only. Any other reproduction or redistribution is strictly prohibited. All rights reserved.
This content is provided for test preparation purposes only and does not imply an endorsement by Mometrix of any particular political, scientific, or religious point of view.

90. B: A main role of a newspaper advisor is to arbitrate disputes among staffers and maintain camaraderie within the staff. Option A, to eliminate the editor's position, is an overreaction to a relatively minor dispute, and the lack of an editor could result in a loss of vision for the newspaper. Option B, to set up a meeting with all three students, is a smarter strategy and one that will enable the students to learn to work out conflicts themselves. Option C, to remind the reporters of the editor's right to maintain a clear vision for the newspaper, may follow the letter of the law, but will ultimately not ease the discord within the staff. The dispute should be solved in order to maintain a harmonious staff. Option D, to redelegate the editor's responsibilities to another student, is an overreaction and one that takes sides, which should be avoided by a good advisor. Option B, therefore, is the best answer choice.

91. A: While the newspaper does have the right to publish without prior review, it is also important to maintain good relations with the administration. Option A, a meeting with the principal, would enable the staff to explain their viewpoint while appearing responsive to the administration's concerns. Option B, an appointment with a lawyer, is an overreaction. Staff should only seek legal advice when other avenues have failed. Option C, an e-mail stating that the op-ed will be published, is within the staff's right, but does nothing to ease relations with the administration. Option D, an abandonment of the op-ed for something more acceptable, is not the best course of action. The staff has the right to publish the op-ed and should not capitulate if it feels the administration does not have a valid educational objection to the planned piece. Option A, therefore, is the best answer choice.

92. C: Student journalists should be exposed to the work and advice of others making a living in the field. Option A, that partnerships with working journalists may help students find jobs, is unrealistic. Most journalism jobs require a college degree. Option B, that it will help students gain access to events requiring press credentials, is also untrue. A student journalist is free to apply for press credentials on her own, and it is unethical to use another's credentials. Option C, that it will enable students to seek advice and mentorship from more experienced journalists, is true. A consultation with a working journalist can be invaluable to a student learning the trade. Option D, that outside partnerships will give student journalists leverage with administration officials, is not true. In addition, student journalists should not think of the administration as an enemy against whom they should strategize. The best answer choice is option C.

93. C: Covering the death of a student, especially in a suicide, must be handled very delicately. Option A, use of anonymous sources, would be unlikely to be a big problem here; at any rate, it is considered ethical to use anonymous sources if, for whatever reason, nobody is willing to speak on the record. Option B, libel, should not cause problems in this case, although a good reporter will always check and double-check his facts to be absolutely sure they are accurate before going to press. Option C, invasion of privacy, could potentially pose problems if the student's family feels that discussing the suicide reveals information they did not want made public. Option D, prior review, is not applicable here. A demand to review the final article before going to press is no more likely to be made than with any other article. Option C, therefore, is the best answer choice.

94. D: It is important for any journalist to maintain neutrality when reporting a story, particularly if he has any kind of relationship with any of the subjects. Option A, to avoid interviewing those closest to the story, is bad advice. A good journalist always gets as close to the source as possible. Option B, to support all his interviews with statistics, is irrelevant; though he may want to supplement the interviews with statistics, many of the interviews are likely to deal with emotional, not statistical, subjects. Option C, to interview as many sources as possible, is a good strategy generally but is not particular to this situation. Option D, to avoid bias in his writing, is the best

Copyright © Mometrix Media. You have been licensed one copy of this document for personal use only. Any other reproduction or redistribution is strictly prohibited. All rights reserved.
This content is provided for test preparation purposes only and does not imply an endorsement by Mometrix of any particular political, scientific, or religious point of view.

advice. Due to the emotional subject and his relationship with the deceased student, the student should strive to avoid any bias in his writing. Option D is the best answer.

95. D: When ethical or style issues arise, a policy should be set for the future. Option A, to include an editorial addressing the problem of suicide, is inappropriate; the solution to their ethical problem was not to mention the suicide, so to mention it instead in an editorial is contradictory. Option B, to invite representatives of the deceased student to comment on the staff's action, is not necessarily helpful. The staff is responsible to the entire readership and must balance competing interests as best it can. Option C, to compile a graph of student-death statistics listing cause of death, may appear callous to readers. Option D, to create a stylebook listing the staff's policy on student deaths, is the best course of action. It will prevent the staff from having to sort out the same problem in the future. Option D is the best choice.

96. A: Photographers' ethics mean never misrepresenting reality. Option A, asking the captain to re-play a shot on goal, is unethical, particularly if the photo's caption in any way allows readers to think this is a photo of the original shot. Option B, cropping the photograph for better composition, is not unethical. Cropping the photograph to intentionally remove elements would be unethical but not for composition purposes. Option C, adjusting the color to increase the contrast, would not necessarily be unethical. Option D, arranging for the captain to pose with a ball, is not unethical; it is obvious that the shot is posed and does not pretend to be otherwise. Option A, therefore, is the most obviously unethical decision and is the best answer choice.

97. B: A photograph that lacks contrast and has a completely white background has likely been overexposed. Option A, to increase the f-stop, adjusts the field of focus and is unrelated to exposure. Option B, decreasing the aperture size, is correct. It would let in less light, resulting in a photograph with more depth and contrast. Option C, to use a telephoto lens, would not affect the exposure but simply allow the photographer to work from a greater distance from the subject. Option D, to use a flash, would not be appropriate, especially when working outside. Option B, therefore, is the best answer choice.

98. D: A good photo caption ties together the story and the photograph. Option A, "Marcus Johnson takes a shot on goal," is not a good caption. A reader should be able to get that information simply from looking at the photograph. Option B, "Marcus Johnson, GHS student," tells the reader almost nothing. A good caption would be more informative. Option C, "Marcus Johnson won a scholarship to Iowa State University. In his spare time, Marcus also likes playing football," adds irrelevant information that does not contribute to the story. Option D, "Marcus Johnson takes a practice shot on goal. Johnson recently won a scholarship to Iowa State University," successfully ties together the article and photo, and is the best answer choice.

99. C: A good two-page spread in a yearbook is visually balanced and draws the reader's interest. Option A, switching the section of student photos with the large photo on the left page, would result in two large photos on the top of both pages, making the spread top-heavy. Option B, switching the two articles with the large photo above them, would make the spread bottom-heavy with small items at the top of both pages. Option C, switching the left-hand article with the left half of the group of student photos, would be a good choice. All text would be on the outer margins, and the spread would be balanced horizontally and vertically. Option D, making each of the articles two columns long rather than one, would result in awkward article format, especially since each of the articles is short. Option C, therefore, is the best answer choice.

100. B: There are roles for many kinds of computer programs in yearbook production, but each serves a specific purpose. Option A, a word processor, is excellent for typing articles, getting word

Copyright © Mometrix Media. You have been licensed one copy of this document for personal use only. Any other reproduction or redistribution is strictly prohibited. All rights reserved.
This content is provided for test preparation purposes only and does not imply an endorsement by Mometrix of any particular political, scientific, or religious point of view.

counts, and running spell check, but it is not the best choice for layout. Option B, desktop publishing software, is designed for laying out photos, text, and graphic elements. It would be a good choice. Option C, photo-manipulation software, is best for adjusting color and cropping photos, but it is not good for laying out many different elements on a page. Option D, a database program, is useful for keeping track of many pieces of information, such as advertising or interview contacts, but would not be good for layout. Option B, therefore, is the best available answer choice.

Copyright © Mometrix Media. You have been licensed one copy of this document for personal use only. Any other reproduction or redistribution is strictly prohibited. All rights reserved.
This content is provided for test preparation purposes only and does not imply an endorsement by Mometrix of any particular political, scientific, or religious point of view.

How to Overcome Test Anxiety

Just the thought of taking a test is enough to make most people a little nervous. A test is an important event that can have a long-term impact on your future, so it's important to take it seriously and it's natural to feel anxious about performing well. But just because anxiety is normal, that doesn't mean that it's helpful in test taking, or that you should simply accept it as part of your life. Anxiety can have a variety of effects. These effects can be mild, like making you feel slightly nervous, or severe, like blocking your ability to focus or remember even a simple detail.

If you experience test anxiety—whether severe or mild—it's important to know how to beat it. To discover this, first you need to understand what causes test anxiety.

Causes of Test Anxiety

While we often think of anxiety as an uncontrollable emotional state, it can actually be caused by simple, practical things. One of the most common causes of test anxiety is that a person does not feel adequately prepared for their test. This feeling can be the result of many different issues such as poor study habits or lack of organization, but the most common culprit is time management. Starting to study too late, failing to organize your study time to cover all of the material, or being distracted while you study will mean that you're not well prepared for the test. This may lead to cramming the night before, which will cause you to be physically and mentally exhausted for the test. Poor time management also contributes to feelings of stress, fear, and hopelessness as you realize you are not well prepared but don't know what to do about it.

Other times, test anxiety is not related to your preparation for the test but comes from unresolved fear. This may be a past failure on a test, or poor performance on tests in general. It may come from comparing yourself to others who seem to be performing better or from the stress of living up to expectations. Anxiety may be driven by fears of the future—how failure on this test would affect your educational and career goals. These fears are often completely irrational, but they can still negatively impact your test performance.

Elements of Test Anxiety

As mentioned earlier, test anxiety is considered to be an emotional state, but it has physical and mental components as well. Sometimes you may not even realize that you are suffering from test anxiety until you notice the physical symptoms. These can include trembling hands, rapid heartbeat, sweating, nausea, and tense muscles. Extreme anxiety may lead to fainting or vomiting. Obviously, any of these symptoms can have a negative impact on testing. It is important to recognize them as soon as they begin to occur so that you can address the problem before it damages your performance.

The mental components of test anxiety include trouble focusing and inability to remember learned information. During a test, your mind is on high alert, which can help you recall information and stay focused for an extended period of time. However, anxiety interferes with your mind's natural processes, causing you to blank out, even on the questions you know well. The strain of testing during anxiety makes it difficult to stay focused, especially on a test that may take several hours. Extreme anxiety can take a huge mental toll, making it difficult not only to recall test information but even to understand the test questions or pull your thoughts together.

Copyright © Mometrix Media. You have been licensed one copy of this document for personal use only. Any other reproduction or redistribution is strictly prohibited. All rights reserved.
This content is provided for test preparation purposes only and does not imply an endorsement by Mometrix of any particular political, scientific, or religious point of view.

Effects of Test Anxiety

Test anxiety is like a disease—if left untreated, it will get progressively worse. Anxiety leads to poor performance, and this reinforces the feelings of fear and failure, which in turn lead to poor performances on subsequent tests. It can grow from a mild nervousness to a crippling condition. If allowed to progress, test anxiety can have a big impact on your schooling, and consequently on your future.

Test anxiety can spread to other parts of your life. Anxiety on tests can become anxiety in any stressful situation, and blanking on a test can turn into panicking in a job situation. But fortunately, you don't have to let anxiety rule your testing and determine your grades. There are a number of relatively simple steps you can take to move past anxiety and function normally on a test and in the rest of life.

Physical Steps for Beating Test Anxiety

While test anxiety is a serious problem, the good news is that it can be overcome. It doesn't have to control your ability to think and remember information. While it may take time, you can begin taking steps today to beat anxiety.

Just as your first hint that you may be struggling with anxiety comes from the physical symptoms, the first step to treating it is also physical. Rest is crucial for having a clear, strong mind. If you are tired, it is much easier to give in to anxiety. But if you establish good sleep habits, your body and mind will be ready to perform optimally, without the strain of exhaustion. Additionally, sleeping well helps you to retain information better, so you're more likely to recall the answers when you see the test questions.

Getting good sleep means more than going to bed on time. It's important to allow your brain time to relax. Take study breaks from time to time so it doesn't get overworked, and don't study right before bed. Take time to rest your mind before trying to rest your body, or you may find it difficult to fall asleep.

Along with sleep, other aspects of physical health are important in preparing for a test. Good nutrition is vital for good brain function. Sugary foods and drinks may give a burst of energy but this burst is followed by a crash, both physically and emotionally. Instead, fuel your body with protein and vitamin-rich foods.

Also, drink plenty of water. Dehydration can lead to headaches and exhaustion, especially if your brain is already under stress from the rigors of the test. Particularly if your test is a long one, drink water during the breaks. And if possible, take an energy-boosting snack to eat between sections.

Along with sleep and diet, a third important part of physical health is exercise. Maintaining a steady workout schedule is helpful, but even taking 5-minute study breaks to walk can help get your blood pumping faster and clear your head. Exercise also releases endorphins, which contribute to a positive feeling and can help combat test anxiety.

When you nurture your physical health, you are also contributing to your mental health. If your body is healthy, your mind is much more likely to be healthy as well. So take time to rest, nourish your body with healthy food and water, and get moving as much as possible. Taking these physical steps will make you stronger and more able to take the mental steps necessary to overcome test anxiety.

Copyright © Mometrix Media. You have been licensed one copy of this document for personal use only. Any other reproduction or redistribution is strictly prohibited. All rights reserved.
This content is provided for test preparation purposes only and does not imply an endorsement by Mometrix of any particular political, scientific, or religious point of view.

Mental Steps for Beating Test Anxiety

Working on the mental side of test anxiety can be more challenging, but as with the physical side, there are clear steps you can take to overcome it. As mentioned earlier, test anxiety often stems from lack of preparation, so the obvious solution is to prepare for the test. Effective studying may be the most important weapon you have for beating test anxiety, but you can and should employ several other mental tools to combat fear.

First, boost your confidence by reminding yourself of past success—tests or projects that you aced. If you're putting as much effort into preparing for this test as you did for those, there's no reason you should expect to fail here. Work hard to prepare; then trust your preparation.

Second, surround yourself with encouraging people. It can be helpful to find a study group, but be sure that the people you're around will encourage a positive attitude. If you spend time with others who are anxious or cynical, this will only contribute to your own anxiety. Look for others who are motivated to study hard from a desire to succeed, not from a fear of failure.

Third, reward yourself. A test is physically and mentally tiring, even without anxiety, and it can be helpful to have something to look forward to. Plan an activity following the test, regardless of the outcome, such as going to a movie or getting ice cream.

When you are taking the test, if you find yourself beginning to feel anxious, remind yourself that you know the material. Visualize successfully completing the test. Then take a few deep, relaxing breaths and return to it. Work through the questions carefully but with confidence, knowing that you are capable of succeeding.

Developing a healthy mental approach to test taking will also aid in other areas of life. Test anxiety affects more than just the actual test—it can be damaging to your mental health and even contribute to depression. It's important to beat test anxiety before it becomes a problem for more than testing.

Study Strategy

Being prepared for the test is necessary to combat anxiety, but what does being prepared look like? You may study for hours on end and still not feel prepared. What you need is a strategy for test prep. The next few pages outline our recommended steps to help you plan out and conquer the challenge of preparation.

Step 1: Scope Out the Test

Learn everything you can about the format (multiple choice, essay, etc.) and what will be on the test. Gather any study materials, course outlines, or sample exams that may be available. Not only will this help you to prepare, but knowing what to expect can help to alleviate test anxiety.

Step 2: Map Out the Material

Look through the textbook or study guide and make note of how many chapters or sections it has. Then divide these over the time you have. For example, if a book has 15 chapters and you have five days to study, you need to cover three chapters each day. Even better, if you have the time, leave an extra day at the end for overall review after you have gone through the material in depth.

If time is limited, you may need to prioritize the material. Look through it and make note of which sections you think you already have a good grasp on, and which need review. While you are studying, skim quickly through the familiar sections and take more time on the challenging parts.

Copyright © Mometrix Media. You have been licensed one copy of this document for personal use only. Any other reproduction or redistribution is strictly prohibited. All rights reserved.
This content is provided for test preparation purposes only and does not imply an endorsement by Mometrix of any particular political, scientific, or religious point of view.

Write out your plan so you don't get lost as you go. Having a written plan also helps you feel more in control of the study, so anxiety is less likely to arise from feeling overwhelmed at the amount to cover.

Step 3: Gather Your Tools

Decide what study method works best for you. Do you prefer to highlight in the book as you study and then go back over the highlighted portions? Or do you type out notes of the important information? Or is it helpful to make flashcards that you can carry with you? Assemble the pens, index cards, highlighters, post-it notes, and any other materials you may need so you won't be distracted by getting up to find things while you study.

If you're having a hard time retaining the information or organizing your notes, experiment with different methods. For example, try color-coding by subject with colored pens, highlighters, or post-it notes. If you learn better by hearing, try recording yourself reading your notes so you can listen while in the car, working out, or simply sitting at your desk. Ask a friend to quiz you from your flashcards, or try teaching someone the material to solidify it in your mind.

Step 4: Create Your Environment

It's important to avoid distractions while you study. This includes both the obvious distractions like visitors and the subtle distractions like an uncomfortable chair (or a too-comfortable couch that makes you want to fall asleep). Set up the best study environment possible: good lighting and a comfortable work area. If background music helps you focus, you may want to turn it on, but otherwise keep the room quiet. If you are using a computer to take notes, be sure you don't have any other windows open, especially applications like social media, games, or anything else that could distract you. Silence your phone and turn off notifications. Be sure to keep water close by so you stay hydrated while you study (but avoid unhealthy drinks and snacks).

Also, take into account the best time of day to study. Are you freshest first thing in the morning? Try to set aside some time then to work through the material. Is your mind clearer in the afternoon or evening? Schedule your study session then. Another method is to study at the same time of day that you will take the test, so that your brain gets used to working on the material at that time and will be ready to focus at test time.

Step 5: Study!

Once you have done all the study preparation, it's time to settle into the actual studying. Sit down, take a few moments to settle your mind so you can focus, and begin to follow your study plan. Don't give in to distractions or let yourself procrastinate. This is your time to prepare so you'll be ready to fearlessly approach the test. Make the most of the time and stay focused.

Of course, you don't want to burn out. If you study too long you may find that you're not retaining the information very well. Take regular study breaks. For example, taking five minutes out of every hour to walk briskly, breathing deeply and swinging your arms, can help your mind stay fresh.

As you get to the end of each chapter or section, it's a good idea to do a quick review. Remind yourself of what you learned and work on any difficult parts. When you feel that you've mastered the material, move on to the next part. At the end of your study session, briefly skim through your notes again.

But while review is helpful, cramming last minute is NOT. If at all possible, work ahead so that you won't need to fit all your study into the last day. Cramming overloads your brain with more information than it can process and retain, and your tired mind may struggle to recall even

Copyright © Mometrix Media. You have been licensed one copy of this document for personal use only. Any other reproduction or redistribution is strictly prohibited. All rights reserved.
This content is provided for test preparation purposes only and does not imply an endorsement by Mometrix of any particular political, scientific, or religious point of view.

previously learned information when it is overwhelmed with last-minute study. Also, the urgent nature of cramming and the stress placed on your brain contribute to anxiety. You'll be more likely to go to the test feeling unprepared and having trouble thinking clearly.

So don't cram, and don't stay up late before the test, even just to review your notes at a leisurely pace. Your brain needs rest more than it needs to go over the information again. In fact, plan to finish your studies by noon or early afternoon the day before the test. Give your brain the rest of the day to relax or focus on other things, and get a good night's sleep. Then you will be fresh for the test and better able to recall what you've studied.

Step 6: Take a Practice Test

Many courses offer sample tests, either online or in the study materials. This is an excellent resource to check whether you have mastered the material, as well as to prepare for the test format and environment.

Check the test format ahead of time: the number of questions, the type (multiple choice, free response, etc.), and the time limit. Then create a plan for working through them. For example, if you have 30 minutes to take a 60-question test, your limit is 30 seconds per question. Spend less time on the questions you know well so that you can take more time on the difficult ones.

If you have time to take several practice tests, take the first one open book, with no time limit. Work through the questions at your own pace and make sure you fully understand them. Gradually work up to taking a test under test conditions: sit at a desk with all study materials put away and set a timer. Pace yourself to make sure you finish the test with time to spare and go back to check your answers if you have time.

After each test, check your answers. On the questions you missed, be sure you understand why you missed them. Did you misread the question (tests can use tricky wording)? Did you forget the information? Or was it something you hadn't learned? Go back and study any shaky areas that the practice tests reveal.

Taking these tests not only helps with your grade, but also aids in combating test anxiety. If you're already used to the test conditions, you're less likely to worry about it, and working through tests until you're scoring well gives you a confidence boost. Go through the practice tests until you feel comfortable, and then you can go into the test knowing that you're ready for it.

Test Tips

On test day, you should be confident, knowing that you've prepared well and are ready to answer the questions. But aside from preparation, there are several test day strategies you can employ to maximize your performance.

First, as stated before, get a good night's sleep the night before the test (and for several nights before that, if possible). Go into the test with a fresh, alert mind rather than staying up late to study.

Try not to change too much about your normal routine on the day of the test. It's important to eat a nutritious breakfast, but if you normally don't eat breakfast at all, consider eating just a protein bar. If you're a coffee drinker, go ahead and have your normal coffee. Just make sure you time it so that the caffeine doesn't wear off right in the middle of your test. Avoid sugary beverages, and drink enough water to stay hydrated but not so much that you need a restroom break 10 minutes into the

Copyright © Mometrix Media. You have been licensed one copy of this document for personal use only. Any other reproduction or redistribution is strictly prohibited. All rights reserved.
This content is provided for test preparation purposes only and does not imply an endorsement by Mometrix of any particular political, scientific, or religious point of view.

test. If your test isn't first thing in the morning, consider going for a walk or doing a light workout before the test to get your blood flowing.

Allow yourself enough time to get ready, and leave for the test with plenty of time to spare so you won't have the anxiety of scrambling to arrive in time. Another reason to be early is to select a good seat. It's helpful to sit away from doors and windows, which can be distracting. Find a good seat, get out your supplies, and settle your mind before the test begins.

When the test begins, start by going over the instructions carefully, even if you already know what to expect. Make sure you avoid any careless mistakes by following the directions.

Then begin working through the questions, pacing yourself as you've practiced. If you're not sure on an answer, don't spend too much time on it, and don't let it shake your confidence. Either skip it and come back later, or eliminate as many wrong answers as possible and guess among the remaining ones. Don't dwell on these questions as you continue—put them out of your mind and focus on what lies ahead.

Be sure to read all of the answer choices, even if you're sure the first one is the right answer. Sometimes you'll find a better one if you keep reading. But don't second-guess yourself if you do immediately know the answer. Your gut instinct is usually right. Don't let test anxiety rob you of the information you know.

If you have time at the end of the test (and if the test format allows), go back and review your answers. Be cautious about changing any, since your first instinct tends to be correct, but make sure you didn't misread any of the questions or accidentally mark the wrong answer choice. Look over any you skipped and make an educated guess.

At the end, leave the test feeling confident. You've done your best, so don't waste time worrying about your performance or wishing you could change anything. Instead, celebrate the successful completion of this test. And finally, use this test to learn how to deal with anxiety even better next time.

Review Video: Test Anxiety
Visit mometrix.com/academy and enter code: 100340

Important Qualification

Not all anxiety is created equal. If your test anxiety is causing major issues in your life beyond the classroom or testing center, or if you are experiencing troubling physical symptoms related to your anxiety, it may be a sign of a serious physiological or psychological condition. If this sounds like your situation, we strongly encourage you to seek professional help.

Copyright © Mometrix Media. You have been licensed one copy of this document for personal use only. Any other reproduction or redistribution is strictly prohibited. All rights reserved.
This content is provided for test preparation purposes only and does not imply an endorsement by Mometrix of any particular political, scientific, or religious point of view.

Online Resources

Due to our efforts to try to keep this book to a manageable length, we've created a link that will give you access to all of your online resources:

mometrix.com/resources719/osatjourn137

It's Your Moment, Let's Celebrate It!

Share your story @mometrixtestpreparation

Copyright © Mometrix Media. You have been licensed one copy of this document for personal use only. Any other reproduction or redistribution is strictly prohibited. All rights reserved.
This content is provided for test preparation purposes only and does not imply an endorsement by Mometrix of any particular political, scientific, or religious point of view.